D1025112

HOME PLACE

THE STORY
OF
THE U.S. HOUSE
OF
REPRESENTATIVES

Books by William S. White

The Taft Story

Citadel: The Story of the U.S. Senate

Majesty and Mischief:
A Mixed Tribute to F.D.R.

The Professional: Lyndon B. Johnson

Home Place: The Story of
the U.S. House of Representatives

HOME PLACE

THE STORY
OF
THE U.S. HOUSE
OF
REPRESENTATIVES

WILLIAM S. WHITE

HOUGHTON MIFFLIN COMPANY BOSTON

The Riverside Press Cambridge

1965

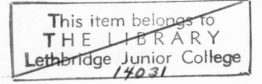
FIRST PRINTING C

To the memory of
Archibald Wade White,
my grandfather,
and John VanDyke White,
my father

CONTENTS

I THE TONE

    1 THE MEMBERS   3

    2 A VIEW FROM THE GALLERIES   11

    3 STEALTHY STATESMANSHIP   18

    4 THE MANY AND THE FEW   28

    5 THE WAY TO SUCCESS   34

    6 SOMETIMES THEY STAMPEDE   43

II THE TYPES

    7 THE LOCALS   53

    8 FREE RIDERS AND NATIONALS   59

    9 SOME PERSONALITIES   64

    10 MAKERS OF SYNTHESIS   72

    11 THE SPEAKER   80

III THE CENTERS AND USES OF POWER

    12 THE COMMITTEES   89

    13 MEN OF INFLUENCE   94

    14 SENIORITY   100

15 "RULES" 108

16 THE OTHER GREAT COMMITTEES 118

IV THE STRENGTHS AND THE WEAKNESSES

17 THE HOUSE AND THE WHITE HOUSE 131

18 FOREIGN POLICY 136

19 THE SENATE MAN IN THE HOUSE 142

20 EFFECTIVE MANEUVER 148

21 CHECKS AND BALANCES 153

22 THE REFORMERS 159

INDEX 171

I

THE TONE

1

THE MEMBERS

THOUGH the long shadows of History throw an occasional grandeur about it, the first and most vital and the last and truest words for the House of Representatives of the United States of America are these: It is an earthy, and earnest and often a dull commonplace which is something larger and finer than mere mediocrity but also something smaller and lesser than conscious grace or greatness.

To begin to understand the place as it really is — as it has grown to be — it is necessary first to understand that this is not so much a house, in the sense of having completeness and unity of architecture and design, as it is a congeries of disparate dwellings oddly thrown together under one roof. The roof is the only part of the structure which is entirely common to the whole.

Nor is this House of Representatives truly and exactly representative of the whole country as that country really exists so much as it is representative of interests and sections and attitudes within that country, some of which are still live and real but some of which retain vitality only here, where the long memory of the House will never let the past quite die. In a word, some traditional sections and interests and attitudes are overly represented, in the mathematical sense, and some of the newer sections and interests are under-represented, again in the same mathematical sense.

Here there still exists in fact what is everywhere else only a nostalgic recollection of yesterday — a nation whose back-bone is still made up of the landholder, the farm community, the local merchant, the small town of small business and small banks where the Odd Fellows and Elks and Masons meet on a Saturday night in the hall above the drugstore.

It is not that the urgent concerns of Big Labor, Big Business and urban blocs and forces are not also felt here in the House. These, too, are present and powerfully so; but not with anything like that ultimate power with which they make themselves and their desires felt in every other part of American public life. Urban America has long since encir-cled the American Presidency—though it has not always captured it save when that Presidency is in Democratic Party hands. Urban America has long since moved demand-ingly upon the United States Senate, notwithstanding the endless and vigorous resistance of the small-state Sena-tors. And urban America has for years dominated the mind and purposes of the Supreme Court of the United States.

But small-town and rural America still occupy the inner fortress of the House of Representatives, heavy and insistent as is the urban siege upon it.

In some distant tomorrow that siege will inevitably break through as reapportionment and Congressional redistrict-ing, shifts of population and the demanding waves of reform and change in American life work their will and way at last. For the time being, however, the House is still, in its true inner being, more nearly the home of nineteenth and even in some ways of eighteenth century America than of that America which is well into the sixth decade of the twentieth century. Indeed, it can be said without great exaggeration that should Thomas Jefferson, in one of those miracles in which it is unlikely that he ever put credence, be able to return to Washington tomorrow, the only institution that would not seem surpassingly strange to him would be the House of Representatives.

For the House yet remains an anachronistic embodiment of many things in which he believed so much — the due and proper dominance of agrarian life over city life; the deliberate separation and fragmentation of the Federal power; the primacy of the small over the large, and of local government over central government. Take it as it is today, the House chamber does not, in terms of its human occupants, appear vastly different from the House of a century and a half ago. Here is an agglomeration — the unflattering phrase "motley collection" is not so very far out — of predominantly middle-class, middle-aged, middle-abilitied Americans who together form an almost perfect microcosm of non-urban America.

Here are exactly the kinds of men who make up that large section of American life which is not quite at the top and is very far from the bottom of the social structure. Look out upon the Chamber and your mind's eye sees this member putting on his American Legion hat on Veterans Day (though the members by and large will still call it Armistice Day) and marching down Main Street, that improbably shiny helmet bobbing upon a head gone more than a little bald and the feet slightly out of cadence just as they always were when he led a platoon or company as a citizen-officer in the First or Second World War.

Look again, and see that member back home in Illinois or California or Texas. He lives in a comfortable house, usually in the best of the old sections of town. His law office — to which he may or may not still be attached as a more or less silent partner — takes only civil cases, of course, and usually only those which involve the solid citizens of the community. His insurance agency does not peddle policies in the streets. His automobile sales room, while no General Motors or Ford or Chrysler plant, is still a long way from bankruptcy. Though it will never put his children into the ranks of America's First Families ("moneywise," as he is regrettably apt to say on occasion) his farm or ranch will easily put son and daughter through some good, though usually not Ivy League, college and will marry them off well, complete with a ranch-style house at the end of the honeymoon.

This composite member is a pretty good Democrat or a pretty good Republican; but rarely a desperate partisan. He will automatically stand with his party on all the purely in-stitutional and routine partisan tests that come in the House — whether his party's nominee or the other party's nominee is to be elected Speaker, and so on. He will stand with a President of his own party so far as he thinks he can. But he will not take it too hard when he defects from the White House on this or that issue, as sooner or later he surely will do. He is far from an intellectual; the very word makes him either angry or at least slightly uncomfortable. He is, however, a reasonably intelligent man at the very worst of him and a highly intelligent man, indeed, at the very best of him.

He is adaptable, ingenious, tough-minded, well informed about what he must be informed about, not given to brilliant visions but instantly able on any occasion to tell a hawk from a handsaw — or a phony from a genuine article. He is, therefore, in no sense anti-intellectual; he simply and rightly suspects people who so designate themselves. He is entirely ready to hire a staff assistant who is intellectual both by definition and in fact; even an intellectual whose hair may be far longer than the Congressman's and whose degrees and academic attainments may be both formidable and from places of learning in which the member himself would never care to set foot.

Moreover, he will listen to and heed that staff assistant, to a point, though back home in Oscaloosa he will never advertise his need for such help. Nor will he mention anywhere that nearly all his set speeches, as distinguished from the rare and sometimes anguished ad-lib remarks which hopefully he will toss across the turbulent, uncaring and unhearing floor of the House in what is called "debate," are painstakingly written by that assistant and handed in tremulous pride to a boss who will secretly regard the precious manuscript as one of those burdens which an unaccountable Providence has seen fit to place upon the patient back of that most patient fellow, a member of Congress.

Unless by chance and luck and high talent he is one of the select handful which really signifies in the House and really

runs it, he is exactly this: a most patient fellow who is more
than a mere cog or digit but less than an important force and
entity, in a large, inchoate place where a vast Average
group is in an uneasy but ultimately useful association with
a very small band of far Above Average. He is set apart from
the happy few who make up Above Average by the simple
circumstance that this is the unalterable way of the place. It
is a place where the Few direct the Many, no matter how
often our civics books have told us that this is *the* democratic
forum of American government. It is also a place where the
Few *must* direct the Many if the House itself is to be able to
perform, at last and in its own way, its high assigned functions to help make the laws of the United States and to help,
spur onward or restrain and chivvy the American Presidency.

But he, this Average, is also once more set apart, this time
not from those who by fortune and ability are his hierarchial
superiors but rather from those who are the non-organiza-
tion men, the rebels and pretenders, of the House. These
latter are neither Average nor Above Average. The House
in all its history has always had a few of them; as a salt for
the stew; as currants in the cake; as "troublemakers," from
the sour point of view of the patriarchs; as the philosophers
and heralds of the future, from the happy point of view of
reformers and advanced liberals. This third force I shall call,
for purposes of labeling and convenience, the Non-Average,
the members who are there and yet not quite there.

Look down at the floor again and — moving the eyes very
slowly, for Non-Average is as far from ubiquitous as is he far
from inarticulate or terrified by form and custom — and

you can see Non-Average sitting in a kind of spiritual aloof-
ness in the House he never made but hopes some day to re-
make to something much closer to heart's desire. If he cele-
brates Veterans Day at all, which is very doubtful, he will
not parade down Main Street but will go by rattling sub-
way to the meeting place of the American Veterans Committee or perhaps of Americans for Democratic Action. His
feet will know no cadences; it is his voice and arm which will
be in action. He will propose with vibrant voice the resolutions through which he is determined to alter — now —
some of our national ways — perhaps the processes of a
House which he believes, though wrongly, to operate far
more by guess and by God than upon any rational plan.

Non-Average is neither quite in nor quite out of the stream
of life in the House: and he both glories in and suffers
from his apartness, his aloneness. He is a city fellow, either in
fact or in his sentiments, engrossed with the problems and
thrusts and demands of an increasingly urbanized American
society which House Average does not so much deny as
quietly deplore and with which Above Average copes with a
tired efficiency in which there is more of resignation to, than
glad acceptance of, unavoidable challenge.

Non-Average is usually a young or youngish lawyer, sometimes an academician diverted to elective politics, occasionally a quasi-professional writer but always a reformer and
Liberal, with a capital L. Most of the time he is a Democrat.
Once in the long yesterdays of this House he was in revolt
from the Whigs or was perhaps beginning to think of joining
that new amalgam of progressives, industrialists, Free-Soilers
and religious intolerants which Abraham Lincoln was weld-

ing into something called the Republican Party. But sometimes, now, he is a Republican, though a very odd one, indeed, to the eyes of the Middle Western-cum Yankee Republicans who now form the vast, orthodox Church of their side of the House. When he is a Republican, he is a Republican from some Northern, usually suburban, district which has rejected the orthodoxy of the party because it lives an essentially urban life on urban income and with urban interests but cannot go quite so far as to vote Democratic.

House Non-Average therefore lives in multi-division. He is divided from both Average and Above Average in the institutional and structural life of the House. He is divided within himself as between the New Democraticism and the New Republicanism and further divided because House tradition still keeps apart, to a degree, the most bonafide Republican rebels and the most bonafide Democratic rebels.

Still, Non-Average somehow works his passage, having a mutually tolerant relationship with Average and a rather painful but genuine relationship with Above Average. For Above Average, whatever his private thoughts, must deal in reasonable patience with every interest and group, section and view.

2

A VIEW FROM THE GALLERIES

RETURN now to the public galleries, if you will, to get the sense and smell, the feel and pulse, of this place which is in constitutional theory the First Legislative body of the American Republic, if not actually the first in the government of this nation in all its enterprises, high and low.

On any ordinary, workaday day here is the scene, a thousand times repeated in history, and in essentials no different really in 1964 from what it was in 1854: The Speaker, sitting upon a high dais which is very like a throne but for a lack of plush or ermine, looks down with dispassionate awareness upon a restless throng sitting below him. The majority party is on his right, the minority on his left. Midway back on each side of the aisle are reddish mahogany tables. These are the centers of real activity in the House (for we can overlook the inconsequential buzzings and to-and-froings of the rank and file). These are "the leadership tables." Here sit the men, Republicans confronting Democrats across the center aisle of the House, who are in charge of the proceedings — saving, that is, for the bleak, august Speaker himself upon his mountain of ultimate authority.

Directly in front of and below the Speaker himself is a fairly small, arched area which is the Well of the House. There members come to take their turn delivering such addresses upon the business at hand as are allowed to them under the rules and by the party leaders. In the Well are tired, shrill microphones. These are a small, single and reluctant concession to modernity which the constant noises of this place have long since required, though these crude metallic devices are still much looked down upon as in poor taste, indeed, by that "Other Body," the haughty Senate of the United States, which is just across the axis of the Capitol to the north.

The rules of the House — and they are legion and are made of iron — forbid mention of "the Senate" in this Chamber. A member may go so far as to mention "Another Body," or, daringly, "The Other Body." This stricture upon debate is one of dozens with which the House has bound itself — the same House which, up to about a century ago, was the preferred forum of such great politicians as Madison and Clay when they set out to make their national reputations. The reasons for their choice have vanished with the winds of time. In the eighteenth century the Senate was principally an advisory body of removed aristocrats, rather as is the present House of Lords in England, and the House was the forge and anvil of national policy and national debate. But the great and terrible storms over slavery and States' Rights which portended the War Between the States forever changed the balance: the Senate became the forum of the states; for these, even the most brilliant of House members could not speak authoritatively, their mandate being based upon Congressional Districts *within* the states. From that day forward, the national debating voice of the House became muted.

Back of all the present nexus of power and authority in the House — the dais, the Well, the leadership tables — sit and lounge, or stroll about and gossip, the general run of House members. Some may be attentive at a given moment; and many more inattentive. In dress and manner and attitude they are a singularly unnoticeable, a singularly unremarkable, group of men, just as mostly they were long ago. In his admirable *History of the House of Representatives* Dr. George Galloway of the Library of Congress calls up a no doubt somewhat finicky witness from the year 1805, Augustus Foster, Secretary in the British legation, to make the point far more sharply than really could have been justifiable then or is justifiable now. But what Augustus Foster wrote of the House to his mother, the Duchess of Devonshire, was not wholly wrong then, nor would it be today.

This undoubtedly is a miserable place [said this fastidious and snobbish young Englishman], but the elect of all the states are assembled in it, and really such a gang to have the affairs of an empire wanting little of the size of Russia entrusted to them, makes one shudder. Imagination is dead in this country. Wit is neither to be found nor is it understood among them. All the arts seem to shrink from it, and you hear of nothing but calculation and speculation in money or in politics. . . . People's depth of reading goes no farther than Tom Paine's muddy pamphlets or their muddier political newspapers. In Congress there are about five persons who look like gentlemen. All the rest come in the filthiest dress and

are well off indeed if they look like farmers — but most seem
apothecaries and attorneys. . . .

Taking up this ancient indictment from Augustus Foster
and analyzing it for its quotients of truth and falsity — and
putting aside its obvious forensic exaggerations altogether —
this writer finds as follows, from long personal knowledge of the House in our time:

Item. It is not "the elect of all the States" who are assembled; nor, on the whole, was it ever. Here assembled, rather,
are 435 men (and a few women) who on the whole faithfully
represent and reflect the manners, or lack of them, and the
interests, essentially economic and bread-and-butter, of a
more or less majority of the voting citizens of Congressional
Districts stretching from Alaska to the Gulf of Mexico, not
to mention into the Pacific to Hawaii. It is not that they are
the elect; it is that they are the elected.

Imagination, in any year and in any turn of history, is not
dead in this House. Imagination subsists here; but here
imagination is chained to the real world of what is possible.
And wit, if often of a mordant kind, is surely not absent. For
one example, and mordant it is, go back a few years when
the House had thrown up two of its special and especially
antithetical sports. There was old John Rankin of Mississippi,
a racist of all racists, a tireless defamer of many, notably of
Negroes and Jews. And there was Vito Marcantonio of New
York, a dark, burning, but also humorous little man who
held in fief a New York district made up primarily of Negroes
and Puerto Ricans.

Marcantonio and Rankin, whose mutual quality of distilled extremism made them brothers as racial demagogues — Rankin on the one side and Marcantonio on the other — screamed at each other on every possible occasion through the brassy microphones in the Well of the House. But, foregathering in private, they were known on occasion to trade not insults but rather laughing offers of pacts of mutual aid. "John," so ran a legend which was also a fact, "if you are really in trouble in Mississippi I will publicly attack you there," Marcantonio would say to Rankin. "Vito," Rankin would reply, "you do that and I will return the favor up in Harlem."

"All the arts seem to shrink from it [the House], and you hear of nothing but calculation and speculation in money or in politics." To this count in the indictment the verdict must be, on the whole, "guilty as charged," but with qualifications. There is, of course, endless speculation in politics, for this is the very coin of commerce in this place. And there is much "speculation in money," except that it is, at bottom, speculation about the taking and the spending of the people's money. And, by and large, it is an informed, a reasonable and a prudent speculation. This function, indeed, lies at the heart of the operations of the House, as I shall later show in more detail.

For this Chamber, in the last analysis, is the place where the domestic policies of this nation — all of them resting at last on the taking and the spending — are really made. Not for this House the grand, glittering policies which make war or peace, which create alliances and help shape nuclear testing and the end of nuclear testing and all that. For this House is, legislatively, the home office of American affairs, the humble place where bread-and-butter and dollars-and-cents are the real concerns of men who look sometimes in anger and distaste, but always in unacknowledged envy, at that Other Body down the long marble corridor which joins, but also endlessly separates, the House of Representatives from the Senate of the United States.

So it can be rightly said that if Augustus Foster was an amusing and in some small respects an accurate observer of the House, as it was then and is now, a more distinguished Briton was rather more perceptive. James Bryce, many years after Foster's letter to the Duchess, thus observed:

> Watching the House at work, and talking to the members in the lobbies, an Englishman naturally asks himself how the intellectual quality of the body compares with that of the House of Commons. His American friends have prepared him to expect a marked inferiority. . . . A stranger who has taken literally all he hears is therefore surprised to find so much character, shrewdness, and keen though limited intelligence among the representatives. Their average business capacity did not seem to me below that of members of the House of Commons of 1880-85. True it is that great lights, such as usually adorn the British chamber, are absent; true also that there are fewer men who have received a high education which has developed their tastes and enlarged their horizons. The want of such men depresses the average. . . . In respect of width of view, of capacity for penetrating thought on political problems, representatives are scarcely above the class from which they came, that of second-rate lawyers or farmers, less often merchants or petty manufacturers. They do not pretend to be statesmen in the European sense of the word, for their careers, which have made them smart and active, have given them little opportunity for ac-

quiring such capacities. As regards manners they are not polished, because they have not lived among polished people; yet neither are they rude, for to get on in American politics one must be civil and pleasant. The standard of parliamentary language, and of courtesy generally, has been steadily rising during the last few decades. . . . Scenes of violence and confusion such as occasionally convulse the French chamber, and were common in Washington before the War of Secession, are now unknown.

3

STEALTHY STATESMANSHIP

BUT THIS foreign analysis, too, requires some critical examination, so that the reality of the thing, the true tone of the House, on this very day when I write, or on any other, may be reconciled with so many widely held theories about it. The House, though many have never understood this, is a parliamentary body, but not part of a parliamentary system as these systems are generally known. British critics, and many Americans who have never grasped the irrelevance of attempting to compare the House of Representatives with the House of Commons do not realize that the House is a part of a Federal and not a parliamentary system.

Men who ask why there is disorder here are not aware that "disorder" is not merely inevitable in this place but was built into it. It was meant to be not cooperative or disciplined but, rather, competitive and undisciplined — competitive with the Senate and the Executive Department alike, and undisciplined in the party sense. In Commons, a majority party not only runs the show but *is* the executive government, too. In the House of Representatives there were in fact no parties at all, as such, in the beginning; and even now there are parties largely only in the housekeeping sense and only for limited purposes.

It is necessary that somebody, some party, have the ultimate responsibility for the operation of the place. Thus an official majority assumes control, after a head count as to which party is the more numerous, for the purpose of choosing the hierarchy of the House — the Speaker and the committee chairmen. All these are agents of the House as a whole. But the majority and minority leaderships — floor leaders, whips and so on — are not actually a part of the House government. They are in each case the creatures only of *one part* of the House, the Democratic part or the Republican part.

A member of the House of Commons majority is himself a part of the government, since the majority party *is* the government. A member of the House of Representatives is — a member of the House of Representatives. His essential function is first to represent the people of his district, and second so to conduct that representation that he forwards, so far as may be, the *national* interest of the country. His obligation to his party varies endlessly. In some places and at some times — for example in an urban community like New York where his party is in ultimate control — he is the creature and chosen instrument of his local party. It may or may not follow that his part of the party is obedient to, and under obligation to, the member of that party who happens to be President of the United States. In any event this member — and his circumstances of election put him into a special case in the House — will first be under the discipline of his local organization and only then, possibly, subject to the discipline of the White House.

And many times the obligation to party is so dim as to be in practical effect nonexistent. Many Southern members, many midwestern members, many New England members, run really as old Joe Jones or ole Bill Smith. The label "Republican" is perforce attached in a strongly Republican area; the label "Democratic" in a strongly Democratic area. Thus, constant complaints that House Democrats don't "vote as Democrats" and House Republicans as "Republicans" are based on fundamental illusions, on basic lack of knowledge of the true nature of the House and of the infinitely diverse sources of power of its individual members.

It is for all these reasons that the personal popularity of a President is almost never an asset transferrable to those members of his party who are running for Congress. There is a profound, essential difference between an election of a President and the 435 quite separate and distinct elections which every two years choose the House of Representatives. Causes, issues, motives are, in the case of House elections, diffused and inchoate. All this may trouble the tidy-minded; but the voting public generally is not deeply moved by this ostensible dichotomy in public affairs. The voting public knows what a good many more sophisticated commentators have never grasped: there is a Presidency, and there is a House of Representatives; it is not a case of two peas in a pod, it is a case of two quite different political growths.

True enough, a strong and insistent President can often rally a majority of his party in the House to vote his way on a given issue. But he does not do it because the party of the

White House has an official majority in the House, or because a party majority in the House should or does mean a government, or Administration, majority in the House. He is able to do it for a whole list of mixed reasons. The bill in question may be generally and reasonably to the taste of his more or less partisan associates in the House. It may be that a decisive majority of them either accept it in the first place or are at any rate not fundamentally opposed to it. And they like to be faithful Democrats or Republicans as far as they can be (if only to avoid being called "bolters"), but not to the point of surrendering their district and personal interests.

Moreover, the power of any President to punish party dissidents in the House — in either party and at any time — is most debatable. Attempted White House "purges" are notable mainly for their spectacular lack of success. And the principal reason lies in that human condition of a member of Congress which is both his principal strength and his principal weakness. The fact that he is an essentially local official, though sent off to a far place called Washington, makes him, uniquely among all functionaries holding Federal power, a home boy and a home choice. This circumstance heavily arms him against high-level reprisals; for the same voters who may madly love a President will turn very cross with him indeed if he reaches down into their district against a Congressman, even one toward whom their feelings of affection may up to this time have been lukewarm.

This circumstance weakens the member in any statesman's role to which he may aspire, for the simple reason that he is a home boy because his first duty is to look after the people at home. Men rarely become known as statesmen because they contend successfully for more Federal money for the dam over Elm Creek and cry out in pain and horror to stay the unfeeling Federal hand which is about to close the Federal testing station at Smithtown or to shut down Camp This or That at Johnsonville.

Still, statesmen do arise in the House of today as they have arisen in every House in all its long history. They do arise — the very few who make up Above Average — in part because they have managed to stay in the House long enough to accumulate adequate seniority to be able to help shape great affairs as well as small. Most important, they find and exploit a rare personal capacity to balance local and national interest so exquisitely as to serve the first adequately for personal survival and the second so well and even so brilliantly as to deserve a national attention and gratitude they almost never receive.

It is this odd, grudging opportunity which the House offers for what might be called a stealthy statesmanship — a national statesmanship hidden from public view under the surface of parochial tasks permitting parochial survival — which alone makes this a truly national House, serving national and world interests as well as local or regional concerns. A great man in the House is a great man, indeed, for many reasons: Because with the best of luck it takes so very long to achieve such stature; because the chance of even starting on the way is very thin in so large and, relative to the Senate, so anonymous and amorphous a body. And, even once there, a man must not seem too aware of his success and his eminence. The House, most of whose members are definitely underprivileged in terms of public distinction, appreciation, esteem or renown, is mortally quick to smell out and ostracize a mere arrivist or opportunist and almost as quick to cut down to size a genuine arriver if he preens himself unduly upon his success.

The House is, on the common surface on which most members always move, desperately egalitarian in its attitudes. On the Senate side of the Capitol, for a small illustration of a big fact about human attitudes, some elevators are reserved exclusively for Senators, at all hours, even when the Senate may not be in session, and all elevators are instantly in the service of Senators whenever one of them may three times press the buzzer. On such an occasion the elevator, even if headed for the top floor with a cargo of visitors, press men or whatnot, will instantly halt its course and go to that floor to which the bell has summoned it. In the House no elevator whatever is exclusively and always assigned to members — though one is labeled "For Members and the Press" — and the most senior member of the House would not dare direct it to go up when the majority within it happened to be going down.

At the end of the Second World War, when there was so much earnestly deploring talk about the horrors of "caste" in a military system wherein officers ate apart from enlisted men and took their most personal errands to different latrines, a military officer called Dwight D. Eisenhower was in the Senate side of the Capitol on business with the great Speaker Sam Rayburn of Texas. Rayburn, in those days, was "Mr. Sam" to Eisenhower—this being, by the way, the origin of a title later generally applied to the Speaker—and Eisenhower to Rayburn was "Captain Ike."

They had pressed the button for a Senate elevator. The

cage stopped for them, hesitated a moment and then shot off afrightedly. "What the . . ." Eisenhower exclaimed. "Some Senator buzzed," said Rayburn. "It's a Senate custom, Captain Ike." Eisenhower turned on the lambent beam of the country's most famous smile and said: "Ah, I see, Mr. Sam. Caste system, eh?"

Again a trifling matter that tells much about tones and shades and attitudes. Any old-timer around the Capitol will go to the Senate restaurant if he wants a fairly dim lunch, served with decorum and some aplomb. But he will go to the House restaurant if he wants a good, hearty beefsteaky meal flung casually at him — and at each and every member who may on that occasion be himself having lunch — by a waiter who has seen many come and go and is as innocent of awe as of punctilio.

In far more significant matters concerning the life of the House the position is much the same. The House is, compared to the Senate, in a sense a barracks as compared to an officers' club, and this is true in the big things as well as in the very little. A man who cuts his way through to the top — and the real top is not always the ostensible top — must reconcile himself to spending enormous devotion, enormous labor at the grinding routine of the place, and to a striking lack of either public awareness or public interest in his life and career. Service in the House is an enterprise in which to a very large extent virtue is its own reward.

This, again for a military metaphor, is a place for the foot-slogger politician and not for "Fancy Dans," an epithet once applied to the Navy before a pleased and understanding House committee by the old infantryman General Omar

Bradley. Prima donnas there are; but primas donnas only inside themselves. Great orators rarely appear in that rigidly regulated thing called House debate, an exercise nearly always totally controlled as to duration and scope by the party leaders sitting in gloomy watchfulness at the little tables while the Speaker scowls down to control *them*. Once granted his little bit of speaking time—five minutes, two minutes, even sometimes one minute — by his party leadership, the thin, *rrr*ing voice of a Yankee may utter a thought or a line that might in other circumstances be memorable and even moving. But instantly he is interrupted by the nasal bellow of some dissident Midwesterner: "Will the Gentleman yield?" The "Gentleman" — and on this old-fashioned and usually quite empty mode of address the House still insists, faithful as always to its massive accretion of rules — will "yield" to some caveat, criticism or rebuttal, and his midwestern critic will destroy whatever is left both of his precious "time" and of the theme and the style he had set for it.

It is true that a member may obtain from the Speaker a "special order," meaning a permission to speak at considerable length. But this he can do only on those days and at those hours when nothing else is afoot in the House; when there is neither debate nor issue before the body. His "special order," therefore, serves solely to permit him to get something off his chest, something which he hurls through the microphone to an unlistening, unpeopled House for the single practical purpose of seeing his prose embedded next day in the *Congressional Record*.

Persuasion is not a part of the art or style of the House,

though on rare occasions it may be applied with some effect by a speech from the Well delivered by a party leader or, very rarely indeed, by the Speaker himself descending from his aloof height to become both the monitor and chief of both sides of the House and the ultimate leader — as he is — of his own party.

The true and climactic legislative process in the House does not depend upon any strength of appeal and counter-appeal on the floor. Rather it arises from the skill and the labor and massive information of the senior people, on both sides of the aisle, who are members of the committee which has had an issue initially in its charge, and has explored it all, head to toe and backways and sideways, in endless committee sessions. Thus it follows that what this old House really is, at the end of it all, is a place for negotiation and settlement, not for debate and deliberation, as is the Senate.

And settlers and negotiators are not necessarily, or even usually, men of special eloquence or commanding personal presence. They are usually, as they are in this Chamber, men who know the facts of a complicated case; working men who are respected for their knowledge, heeded for their long demonstrated skill, and neither loved nor hated but only accepted for what they are — the authorities in the matter.

Let your mind's eye fall for a moment upon a typical situation in the House. Here is a bill dealing, say, with social security. Taxes are involved in it. Budgets are involved in it. Compassion is involved in it, but prudent men will want prudence to be involved in it, too, and so prudence will be. Politics, of course, is always involved in it; but often not so much or so deeply involved as most people think. For, coming down to the kernel of the thing, what is most of all involved is great complexity. And of the thousands of bills introduced into the House in any session, no member of Average (and no member even of Above Average) can possibly have much personal knowledge. Even if he be willing to accept the simple dictates of his party, assuming his party has taken a partisan position on the matter, he must have some guidance beyond this. After all, he may later be required to explain the vote he is about to cast; it is wise to have a pretty good idea of what the bill is really about, all partisan cries and countercries notwithstanding. For the most damaging possible gaffe in the politics of the House, as anywhere else, is to have to say: "I really don't know."

4

THE MANY AND THE FEW

So FROM one of the leadership tables there rises some plain, undistinguished-looking fellow who sets out to explain for the majority party what this bill is about. This he does without nonsense; without that rich, if often beautifully underplayed, sense of drama and theater that so often enlivens that "Other Body" down the long white corridor. This fellow cannot afford nonsense; first because there is no time for it; second because the House has no stomach for it, being so niggardly with "time" to anybody and everybody; and third because nonsense will only burden his job, which is difficult enough already.

A similarly unremarkable fellow from the minority leadership table takes his turn, recounting his objections, dissecting the bill, making sad eyes over his prognosis as he shows its clinical weaknesses, or perhaps villainies. It may be that most of the House will not seem to listen much to either of the leaders. The position, however, is not so bad as it looks; for every House member has, or can have, a full printed report of everything of any validity which can possibly be said

about the bill, either way. It has all been said and said
again, in the committee hearings. And the meat of it is given
in this printed report and summary.

What now follows is, usually, a grave, traditional charade.
The House drones on to a result that, usually, has long
been foretold. The conclusion here is easily predictable;
passage of the bill will lie at the end of this road nine times
out of ten. For nine times out of ten, bills on major subjects
do not get to the House floor in the first place unless a fairly
approving consensus has already been assured, in the long
work in committee and then in the constant ear-to-ear and
shoulder-to-shoulder negotiation and discussion between
parties and between members. Rarely, the approving consensus will be strictly partisan. Generally, when the Democrats control the House, it is simply a consensus formed of
many Democrats and some Republicans. Generally, it is
simply a consensus formed of many Republicans and some
Democrats, in times when Republicans control the House.
On extraordinary occasions the Democrats may be solidly
on one side and the Republicans solidly on the other. But
these occasions arise so seldom that for all practical purposes it may be said that the parties will vote strictly as
monolithic parties only as to which party is to control the
offices and housekeeping mechanisms of the House.

For what forever occurs down on the floor of this House is
only in a small sense a contest for supremacy between parties
as such.

Of course, there have been historically brief aberrations,
such as occurred in Franklin D. Roosevelt's time, when the
House has fallen into the hands of a majority so massive as

to make almost meaningless altogether that dividing aisle which at least ostensibly separates the parties. In those moments the aisle has become for all practical purposes altogether obliterated. But the House, like all human institutions, lives by and must be measured by the ordinary realities of its history. So almost always the contest on its floor is a contest for the mind and purposes of the House between two small and able sets of Above Average — Democratic and Republican. These two sets of the few Above Average lead, inform, mildly hector and generally shepherd the great many Average, who though never wholly docile are nevertheless almost never prepared to strike out on their own in making those final legislative decisions which become Acts of Congress.

This is no case of mere bovine docility. It is only a reflection of the basic reality that while the House, taking it in the whole, is a large place, it is at its decisive center a small forum in which a handful of extraordinary men must, and do, lead a great clutch of ordinary men. Nor is this circumstance merely a reflection of the high complexities of modern living in an era of great industrial, social, racial, political and foreign policy tensions. The very first Congress found in 1789 that its business could not go forward except on the principle that the peoples' Representatives must themselves submit to a form of representative government in their own House. The many found it impossible to avoid delegating a good deal of their own responsibility and authority to the few who were in position really to examine this or that specific issue before Congress.

This did not mean then, and it does not mean now, that

the generality of the House surrendered its ultimate authority. But it meant that in necessarily handing over to smaller groups the vital task of making the initial inquiry into any given issue, the generality of the House hands over to the few the enormous opportunity to become much more rationally informed, and to that degree much more rationally decisive.

This vital and unavoidable circumstance has made and molded, all through the years, the true, inner character of the House itself. That true character is vastly different from the common stereotypes about the House. Because its members are elected every two years, and the Senate's only every six years, legend has it that the House is both the more "democratic" in practice and the more readily responsive to national popular opinion and will. The truth is to the contrary. For while all the House is up before the voters every two years, no single member, contrary to the situation in the Senate, is *ever* up before any large number of voters, speaking in national terms. Moreover the House is in no sense "democratic" in its inner functioning, if "democratic" be taken to mean that a mere head count can ever alone determine its direction.

And it is usually (and I believe this to have been the case all through history) more nearly responsive to what may be wanted by the controlling majorities of voters in a fairly small number of key districts than to what may be wanted by a national consensus. The operative phrase here is "key districts," for it is these districts which habitually and traditionally provide that small but infinitely important section of "safe" seats from which members may accumulate, year upon year, and Congress after Congress, that seniority of service which is the core of ultimate House power. It is a power so great that, most of the time and by and large, those who hold it can not merely profoundly influence the tone of the House in action but can also at least shape or reshape, and at most veto and redirect, the initial purposes of the great numerical majority. This is done through an elaborate, complicated and puissant hierarchial structure which has its base in the Rules of the House, its center in the control by seniority of the committee system, and its apex in the high official offices of the House — the Speakership and the major committee chairmanship. The party leadership positions operate roughly in tandem with these offices.

I shall return to this structure later to show in detail its substantive mastery of the House. For present purposes the nature and composition of those key and vital districts requires examination. They are in essentially one-party areas (the South) or in more or less one-party areas (parts of the Middle West, sections of New England). And in a great proportion of cases they are districts where traditional values — and sometimes prejudices—overcome the more modern values. They are, that is to say, commonly "conservative," in the sense that they do not welcome change or innovation. And they are commonly isolated to a degree from what might be called the main streams of current national life.

One does not find many such districts in the great, burgeoning, futuristic states like California. One rarely finds them in any essentially urban area of the country, although they do turn up occasionally in states like New York and Massachusetts to the degree that the old-fashioned urban

Democratic machines like Tammany Hall still possess, here and there, the power to designate and quietly to elect and re-elect and re-elect again some member of Congress. Such an example is currently seen in the extraordinary Negro clergyman Congressman Adam Clayton Powell, whose capacity to return again and again from Harlem has long since placed him in the hierarchy as chairman of the House Labor Committee.

Nor are such districts so easily to be found any more even in that part of the South which is growing rapidly and industrializing even more rapidly. For growth and industrialization and urbanization tend to promote change of all kinds, including political change. Texas, *the* powerhouse, politically, in the South, still holds such districts and no doubt will long do so. Even from Texas, however, the average length of service of any given Congressional delegation will be found to be lower than that of the one which went before it.

5

THE WAY TO SUCCESS

In the Congress which was sitting when I began this book, the Eighty-seventh, six of the most powerful committees of the House (and no more than twelve committees could so be described with realism) were under control of members from just such districts as have been described here. In terms of population, of economic power, and indeed of general political power outside the House itself, all six of these districts put together could be dropped into New York State and lost without trace. Nevertheless, the six members from these districts had a degree of decisive influence in the House which could not have been remotely matched by all the members of the House and both Senators from New York — or, for that matter, by all the members of both Houses from, say, New York, California, Pennsylvania and Illinois all put together.

Now while all this in part simply reflects the nature of the House, it also gives opportunity for a striking illustration of the deep and basic differences in tone between the House as an institution and that "Other Body," the Senate. For power in the Senate comes from seniority, yes; but it also comes from other and far more subtle factors, including personality, forensic skill, and the incomparable forum offered there for more "democratic" individual action — in a place commonly supposed to be far less "democratic" than the House. For while the public no doubt has read a thousand times more about the rules of the Senate than those of the House — and particularly about that famous Senate "Rule XXII," the so-called anti-filibuster rule—the odd fact remains that Senate Rules are by and large only such loose and easy ones as gentlemen might adopt in a club. They stretch with great tolerance—for the right man at the right time—and they bend with great grace, particularly when the common sense of the body commonly senses that some extraordinary and grave matter is at hand and therefore requires extraordinary treatment. If Senate rules are not wholly "democratic" — for example, the great difficulty certainly found by any majority in silencing any determined minority — they are highly liberal and sympathetic to the human personality. Thus they permit the smallest member in terms of influence to raise a devoted public following in his state or even all over the nation, whether or not he can or ever could raise one in the Senate itself, simply by resolute howling upon each and every legislative occasion that may present itself.

But House men live, in this matter, a life of Spartan self-denial. A man cannot become eminent there simply by talking, even assuming his thoughts to be of purest gold and his style and diction and voice of rarest silver. He is a *doing* fellow or he is, in a vulgar phrase, a nothing-man. A great House man may — and habitually one or another in fact does — become infinitely more important to the legislative process and infinitely more vital to public affairs than any dozen lesser members of the Senate. He may and does do all this — but still he will almost never reach, or at any rate has rarely reached since the time just before the Civil War, that pinnacle of public notice and public esteem which nearly any Senator with a good voice and a good "public relations" instinct can readily reach.

In the Eighty-seventh Congress the one man most truly responsible, apart from President Kennedy himself, for a national turn toward free world trade which has had no real parallel in the life of the Republic was a great member of the House named Wilbur Mills from Arkansas. Mills, as chairman of the House Ways and Means Committee, first broke all the way through the ancient ice jam of protectionist sentiment, of "Buy America" and so on, which for a century and a half had forbidden the executive power of this country to deal with any fully flexible authority with the matter of tariffs. (True enough, another onetime member of Congress, Secretary of State Cordell Hull, had cut through the top crust of that ice nearly half a lifetime before, in the first Reciprocal Trade Act. And, fittingly enough, Hull, too, was from one of those key and vital districts which we have discussed, his being in Tennessee.)

Mills, a slightish, compact, markedly quiet man with old-fashioned slicked-down hair and a casual, easy, country-boy attitude, hides enormous political and economic sophistication under an air of having none at all. He brought the Administration's bill safely through, first in the committee and then in the House, in its most desperate test. Some time afterward, when the smoke of battle had died and the victory had been won, I asked a number of ordinarily reasonably well-informed men what they knew of Wilbur Mills, who goes in the House by the old-fashioned, rural-sounding nickname of "Ole Wilbur."

All six of them knew, of course, that he was a Member of Congress from Arkansas. Three of them knew he was chairman of the Committee of Ways and Means. All of them knew he had had some association, vague or otherwise, with the trade bill—which was to be incomparably the greatest achievement of a whole two-year Congress. But only two of them had any real idea of the climactic nature of his contribution to this immense issue. Nor, for that matter, did certain junior members of the very Administration which had asked for this historic bill.

Each and all of my six could have told me everything about, say, Senator Wayne Morse of Oregon, or any one of another half dozen of those legislatively inconsequential but irrepressibly headline-capturing members who always stand at the fringes of the Other Body. There are two principal points to the anecdote. The first is that it is important to understand that Mills is offered here not as Mills but as a type figure of the man of power, of decision and of relative public obscurity who in any session and in any season will be found at the center of affairs in the House. The other is that while attitudinizing, theatrics, the whole bag of tricks of the fellow who talks much and accomplishes little, will profit no man *within* either the House or Senate, that bag of tricks will not profit a House man even *outside* Congress, as it will the Senate man.

The humility of the House, taking it as a whole, has been

one of its outstanding characteristics nearly from the beginning, is so now, and no doubt ever will be. Its own private evaluation of itself implicitly accepts this humility, even through at times it bears upon its institutional shoulder a collective chip which is defensively aggressive in relation to the Senate. This is the case, that is to say, among Average in the House. Above Average, secure in the fact of power as distinguished from its mere appearances, is largely untroubled by envy and largely philosophical about its poor standing in the status myths of public life.

House Average always tends to look with ambitious hope upon the possibility of moving up to the Other Body. Above Average looks at the Other Body with that same cool realism with which it confronts all political issues and all political life. Above Average knows that to trade a place among the untitled elect in the House for a junior Senatorship can well be like kicking oneself up a very elegant but not very interesting flight of gilt-covered stairs.

In the natural order of things, of course, this process of promotion does go on; a fairly high percentage of the roster of the Senate in any given session is made up of ex-House men. Not all of these will have left any great position in the House in the first place; but some will invariably have done so. They will thereafter be content or not content in the Senate primarily on these considerations: whether their basic interests are in domestic or foreign affairs, and whether fortune and circumstance and personal qualities cause them to enter or to be long barred from that imaginary but real place in the life of the Senate which, in another book, I once called the Inner Club.

For if a politician's heart is enchanted with the homely problems: taxes, appropriations, farm legislation and so on, the House is a better place in which to remain — assuming, of course, that he is currently in or has reasonable hopes of shortly entering the hierarchy of the House. If, however, he yearns to tell Khrushchev off, to become truly involved in the great issues of world policy and foreign relations, the Senate will be his true ground. Or rather it is his true ground, given all this, if he can make his way into the *Senate* hierarchy which is the Inner Club.

Acceptability in the hierarchy of the House will not necessarily imply acceptability in that of the Senate. For in no important way are they really alike. The value judgments of the House are based on a quality of perception summarized by that marvelously apt old cliché, "horse sense." The House elevates or holds back a man when in its judgment, after seeing his work in committee, it feels that he has established or failed to show steadiness in the road, competence in pulling his due load, and unshakable doggedness in discharging his often dreary obligations toward whatever salient may be assigned to him of that massive invasion of thousands of proposed bills and resolutions which in every session assaults the minds and spirits and energies of the House as a whole. No amount of Fancy Danism can save the poor fellow if he doesn't do all his work and do it right all the time.

His views, say, upon what to do with Castro and how to handle Southeast Asia may be, and in fact sometimes are, both creative and significant. But this will never help him if, as a member, for instance, of the House Committee on Post

Offices, he doesn't really know, when the time comes, what is in the bill dealing with second-class mailing matter.

The first prerequisite to membership in the House hierarchy, in short, is as simply stated as it is agonizingly hard to attain: high professionalism in the legislative art and process. No such reasonably clear definition could possibly be given of what is required of a man to enter the Inner Club of the Senate. The qualifications there are as gossamer and evanescent as moonlight in autumn; as real and unbending as the New Englander's iron attachment to prudent good taste or the Southerner's indescribably intuitive concepts of what might be called an honorable sense of personal and national responsibility.

The Inner Club of the Senate will neither reject nor later expel an applicant simply because he may be lazy or even not very competent in legislative work. It will not, so long as he is the sort of fellow who in the last crisis of any public affair of great moment will do his duty as he sees it with some grace — and not be either pompously self-satisfied with his own probity and wisdom or screechingly intolerant of the probity and wisdom of his opposition. A kind of instinctive definition of what is a public man's proper gentility is the heart of the unwritten rules of admission here; the Senate Inner Club, a Community of Gentlemen.

But the House has little taste or time for such fine-spun vagaries. To be a member of the Hierarchy there a man need not be either graceful or tolerant, so long as he is reliable and effective. The question as to whether or not he is a screecher hardly arises; there is no time or room in the House for much screeching — and besides, nobody would listen anyhow.

And there is no need for many self-made rules in the way of personal conduct. The embedded and imperious Rules of the House foresee all possible contingencies; they both chain and featherbed the member.

The House hierarchy therefore is in no way a Community of Gentlemen. It is far more like a professional association or labor union of highly skilled workers in which a man's manners are infinitely less important than what he does. His colleagues judge him under the pitiless, objective light of their own shared competence.

All this is not to say that the hierarchy of the House does not sometimes elevate men of incompetence; there is rarely a time when *some* dunderhead is not at the head of *some* committee by the mere inexorable workings of seniority. But it should be emphasized, first, that this is at any rate the exceptional situation, in a chamber having a score of committees, and, second, that membership in the hierarchy, as defined by the committee system is not in every circumstance necessary for the possession of some good degree of second-removed influence. A man of rare excellence — and rare personal connections with those who hold the ultimate power in the House — can make himself felt without ever reaching any formal hierarchial status, though, indeed, this is a most exceptional sort of accomplishment. Occasionally, and here and there, a member can do it by establishing his usefulness to those at the very top of the power structure by becoming their informal and untitled confidant and adviser. To take a recent example, Richard Bolling of Missouri, though neither a member of the House leadership nor yet a committee chairman, was a great power in the days of Speaker Sam Rayburn

of Texas simply because, knowing the mind and purposes
of the Speaker and holding his confidence, he was able to become a kind of untitled minister without portfolio in the
actual governance of the House.

6

SOMETIMES THEY STAMPEDE

THOUGH it has not always been so, the press for many years has been enchanted with the Senate and largely bored with the House. It is a matter of which I personally have rueful knowledge; as a Congressional correspondent in younger days I was unable to bring myself to go to the House when anything at all was doing in the Senate. The reasons for this inattentiveness to the First Chamber are, I believe, several, and unrelated. The first is that the inherently disciplined, unavoidably workaday and usually mercantile hum of the House ill competes with a Senate where almost anything may happen, or be said, at any time. The second is that the House has arbitrarily been driven from the center of the stage in these latter years by the nature of the national political problem.

Three decades ago, under old Speaker John Garner, the House was the focus of interest in an era of domestic economic reform. And economics, bread-and-butter, is, in the last analysis, almost the House's reason for being. There was also the collateral fact that Garner was an able and amiably ruthless politician who, in the House at that time, was cutting President Herbert Hoover to ribbons, amid great national unemployment and distress, and asserting the House's primacy in our economic life as it had not ever before in history been asserted. At that time, the Senate ran a poor second in public notice; but only for a very short time.

What has really happened in these last thirty years is that the true concerns of the American people, beginning with the early crawlings of Hitlerism, have been turned outward from bread-and-butter upon a world of tireless menace. All this has thrown the House into the shadows, for foreign policy is not its job, and correspondingly has cast the great public light upon the Senate.

The press's lack of grateful response to the House in our days is markedly shared by the official hostesses of Washington and, within the purlieus of the United Nations, in New York. And kind of small bureaucrat, especially if he is from the State Department, is welcomed, if not actually seated at the dinner table, before a powerful member of Congress. And yet the Congressman's actual writ in public affairs compares to the bureaucrat's about as that of a Secretary of Defense compares to that of a junior sanitation expert in the Peace Corps. House Average, by and large, is simply not invited anywhere. Above Average, placed spiritually if not actually below the salt, smiles inwardly and keeps his poise, even when some irritating minor member of the Other Body joins the hostess in kindly patronizing him. A sense of proportion, and a wry humor, is taught in the bearpit of the House; in the slang of military service the big fellows are not encouraged to call for the chaplain or the medic when the way is hard and rough.

The Speaker himself will always pull his social weight, even hostesses are aware that the Speaker is next to the President and Vice President as the designated head of this country when and if death should strike them both, but he does not enjoy the underestimation of his men (almost I said "troops," for the Speaker is both an umpire and a Captain over his House) and he surely does not enjoy having the Senate come it over grand with either them or himself. Sam Rayburn carried the dignity of the Speakership to a height it had perhaps not reached since Henry Clay, in part because of a fierce institutional love for and pride in the House. It was, as he himself once put in a moment of private nostalgia, "my life." It was his habit to look with grumpy skepticism on those members who followed ambition's call to the Senate. Far from congratulating one who made the transition to the Other Body, the old gentleman was more likely to speak commiseratingly of him as a good fellow who had unaccountably failed to listen to the voice of reason.

At a time when Lyndon B. Johnson, an old House man, was not only well thought of in the Senate but also had reached the not inconsiderable position of minority leader there, Rayburn spoke to me of our mutual friend as we sat of a late afternoon over a drink in that famous unofficial House club which in Rayburn's time — and in the times of Speakers Nicholas Longworth of Ohio and John Garner of Texas before him — was called The Board of Education.

"You know, Bill, it was a sad thing — no, it was a terrible thing — when ole Lyndon decided to leave here and go over yonder. If he had stayed on here he could have been quite a powerful figure — in a few more years."

The Board of Education met in the most private of the

various offices maintained for the Speaker. It was a small, tucked-away room whose door bore no notice, in which Rayburn habitually met with a few members and perhaps one or two others to chew over a dying day's House business and to plot and plan for some near or far tomorrow. It is not clear who originated its splendid title; to me, it seems most likely, on all the available evidence, that Longworth did.

Rayburn's view, and it was a view which could safely be described as generally the view of the great House men all down through the decades, was that while the House was no doubt put upon and belittled by ignorant men and women as inferior to the Senate, it was the true home of the effective American political process. At heart, he considered the Senate to be something of a pompous nuisance; and at heart he did not really trust its elaborate discussions. Nor would he concede, even in the mellowest of moods, that the Senate debates were of an infinitely higher grade than what passes for debate in the House.

Years ago, about a week after I had published a book called *Citadel: The Story of the U.S. Senate*, I ran into Speaker Rayburn in a corridor of the House. I was a bit pleased with the reception of the book by Senate acquaintances and I was, perhaps not unnaturally, anxious to know what Rayburn would have to say upon the matter. He cocked his head and bowed his massive neck and said with a growl of a certain amiability which all the same was still a growl: "What the hell are *you* doing over on this side of the Capitol?"

Still, the House which was so long his home is not, in fact, quite that unique home of the effective political process

which he believed it to be. It is capable of fast and powerful action — as when, in Franklin Roosevelt's Administration, in the emergencies of the Great Depression, it
passed "bills" which were in fact only rolled-up newspapers,
the actual drafts not having yet come from the printer. No
other part of the American governmental structure, not even
the Presidency, more vindicates the capacity of that government to move with swift decision in crisis. The House is perhaps the most effective proof and symbol of the capacity of
American political leadership really to lead. Given crisis in
our domestic affairs, this place by and large will respond always with heartening celerity — but only sometimes with
reassuring wisdom. Given crisis in our foreign affairs — especially complicated crisis engaging more than ordinarily
the moods and passions of the country — the wise observer
will thank God that there is another place called the United
States Senate. He will also have cause sometimes to utter such
thanks on purely domestic issues, when they intimately touch
upon the ancient Constitutional guarantees to private persons
and private property.

For the urgent processes which move the House have not
been attained and solidified into its institutional life without
accompanying cost. This body which can move so satisfyingly
fast can, upon occasion, also move much too fast indeed; so
fast as to alarm in retrospect even the very ones who
spurred it on. I have seen this body approve a bill to draft
striking railroad workers at the behest of a President named
Harry Truman who, understandably sick with frustration at a
threatening paralysis of transport in wartime, had quite forgotten a document called the Constitution of the United

States. The Senate calmly put the matter aright by simply re-
fusing — under the momentary leadership of such an oddly
mixed pair as Senator Robert A. Taft of Ohio and Senator
Claude Pepper of Florida — to let the measure arise there
at all. This victory for the Constitution and for Liberalism
was achieved in the Senate by a Republican Conservative
and a Democratic ultra-Liberal by resort to the threat of
something which could never occur under the rigid Rules
of the House, a filibuster.

I have seen the House, under processes limiting to perhaps
two hours the total debate of more than four hundred men
on issues of infinite complexity, approve with a great hurrah
manifestos in foreign policy which were unbelievable in their
lack of awareness of the world and which might have all but
destroyed some of our highest foreign enterprises. Again, it
was the Senate which came to the rescue.

For one of the least engaging, but most persistent, habits
of the House is to run wild now and again, not so much over-
throwing its leaders as infecting even them with aberrant
notions and demands. Though these manifestations invariably begin with House Average, there are times when they
are tolerated, if not actually supported, by Above Average.
Indeed, by long tradition one of the unstated but real jobs
of the Senate is to restrain that body which Senate rules do
not forbid anyone to call with forthright simplicity "the
House of Representatives." Not even the most faithful and
industrious statistician or researcher could possibly count
the number of times in history when the Other Body has prevented the House from behaving with surpassing irresponsi-
bility, not to say outright idiocy, on those subtle matters,

again mainly foreign policy matters, with which its massive and generally admirable fact-finding processes are simply not equipped to deal.

In my own experience for a long time, and, I suspect, for the greater part of its whole history, Presidents and Secretaries of State have had to cope with this reality: the House is absolutely vital to their foreign policy designs, since it is generally the initiating place for the necessary appropriations to carry them out; but the House is usually a most doubtful ally beyond this essential but not inspiriting contribution.

For, to repeat, the House is not only the home place in our governmental life; it is also really at home only in the home place.

While I do not pretend to assert this on his authority, I have strong reason to suspect that one of President Kennedy's principal reasons for reluctance to see John W. McCormack of Massachusetts succeed the dead Sam Rayburn in 1962 as Speaker in the Eighty-seventh Congress lay in this essential circumstance. An admirable man, an able man in his way and a faithful partisan, too, McCormack nevertheless seemed, rightly or wrongly, enveloped in an aura of essentially parochial concerns — worthy but still parochial.

II

THE TYPES

7

THE LOCALS

FOR PURPOSES of generalization I have heretofore divided the men (and a few women) of the House of Representatives into Average, Above Average, and Non-Average. Such terms for indicating the large, corporate and institutional facets of the personality of the House are adequate. What is needed now, however, is to depart from a view of the general and to begin to look upon the particular; to cease peering at the whole, round sum and to examine the living roster of the place in its parts.

Elsewhere I have offered the conviction that there is in the Senate an authentic and controlling "Senate type"; a special Man-of-the-Senate who may be said fairly to symbolize, to typify and in the end actually to embody that institution at its work. The House, however, is another tale altogether. A large, diffuse and helter-skelter place, it is in some real senses a masterpiece of that pluralism which has, thus far at least, so long expressed and distinguished both the American society and the American political process. Some would call it "the American Dream"; but the application of any such lofty-precious concept to this essentially hard and sweaty forum of government would offend simple realism and would rightly evoke rude murmurs and jeers from House men, themselves.

Thus, while there is certainly no single "House type" as such, there are, and probably have always been, a good many distinct types. The Senate is singular, in more ways than one; the House is plural, in every possible way. The largest House set properly definable as one type are what I call the locals. These are the fellows who, with varying degrees of candor, come to the Capitol, and stay there, strictly as emissaries of their districts, with no grand delusions that they are "ambassadors," but rather in full awareness that they are the agents of their people almost in the sense that the lobbyists who haunt the committee rooms and House corridors are there to perform the perfectly valid mission of putting forward the views of labor, management, agriculture, or whatnot.

The locals come from everywhere. They see their task as one of representative government in the most intimate and bread-and-potatoes way. They are there to express the wishes of their constituents and to look out for their material interests. After this, they will perform, vaguely or not and consecutively or not, such chores in behalf of such large national or international interests as may, in this order of priorities, come their way. Generally, they are not senior members of the House; generally, therefore, they do not arrive at that point of committee seniority which is requisite to attaining much influence over, or responsibility for, affairs on either a national or an international plane.

They come and they go, for in the nature of things their election will usually depend in the first place upon the short-term desires or problems of voters — to get the Federal dam over Hickory River; to try to alter some local economic imbalance, and so on. Having reached office upon issues that are either transitory or significant solely, or largely, at home, in a deep sense they lack an established, a consecutive and a coherent constituency.

Their life is hard; though it is only what they have chosen. They spend most of their time not upon legislation, either large or small in significance, but rather in running the endless errands of the people back home. They go to the Post Office Department to improve mail deliveries. They are in more or less continuous correspondence with the Department of Defense respecting Johnny's draft status. People at the Interstate Commerce Commission or perhaps the Federal Communications Commission know them well.

For there are always freight rate injustices to adjust; there are television or radio franchises to obtain or to try to obtain for constituents. There are a thousand and one things which must engage the locals' interest and attention as one or another bureau or aspect of the Federal government affects the ordinary citizen's life.

These chores the locals must do; and for what, by almost any measure, are rather meager rewards. A member of the House must have and maintain two places of residence, at home and in Washington. On a salary of $22,500 a year this is not an easy thing; nor is it an easy thing that the family perpetually must live two lives in two homes on two levels. When Congress is in recess the family may be at home in their

Congressional District — this is usually in the summertime. When Congress is in session, and this is always in the wintertime and sometimes through much of the autumn, the children must shuttle between two sets of schools, the wife dragging them and herself back and forth. For everybody — for the member, for his wife, for the children — there is so much to do and there is so very little time in which to do it all.

The locals, therefore, are on many occasions not much better informed personally upon great legislation before the House, wherever it lacks immediate relevancy to the urgent affairs of their own districts, than are the people at home. The disability, however, as I have indicated earlier, is not so great as it looks. For the locals, on such questions, always have at hand the advice and the expertise of the committees, and of the leaders and the senior members of the House in general. And at any rate, when the bells clamor that a vote on the House floor is at hand, the locals can, and do, hurry in from whatever errands have been occupying them, and hear at ear's edge the comforting murmur of an agent of the leadership: "We are voting 'aye.' We are voting 'aye.'" Now, this picture of the locals at work is not an inspiriting one; but it is neither quite so dreary nor quite so denying of the national interest as might at first appear. For the locals have this great virtue: given success in their somewhat piddling tasks of serving their district's interest and its collateral ease of mind, they can, more often than not, vote upon the great issues which come before the House with a certain degree of detachment which helps to cancel out their apparent lack of interest in the matter at hand.

If they cannot help shape the significant legislation of our times, and this, indeed, by and large they cannot do and will not do, they can and often do make that ultimate and most critical of all contributions to it. They can cast the right vote at the right time, and never mind the uncomfortable fact that their reasons, as also their reasoning, may not be of the very best. These fellows also serve; though they only run their errands and wait for the time to weigh in with a vote that is cast more upon trust in the admirable hierarchial committee system of the House than on knowledge of all that may be involved.

There is no special harm in this arrangement; or if there is, there is, quite simply, no alternative to it. The spectacle of the whole membership of the House personally and intimately engaged, all of them and all at once, upon any given matter of importance could not be contemplated by other than fanciful men.

Moreover, there is a second and irreplaceable virtue in the mere existence of the locals. True, the notion of a Member of Congress as solely a messenger for his district can be carried so far as wholly to reject the consideration that this in the end is supposed to be a national instrumentality. But the theory that Congress should be *only* a national instrumentality is wholly inoperative. Nowhere in national government but in the House of Representatives can local interests effectively make themselves continuously heard. Occasionally and sporadically they can be heard in the Senate, mainly through the Senators from the smaller states. But even here the interests of one district may be different from, or actually in conflict with, the interests of the district lying next alongside in the same state. Somebody has got to speak for *one* district, and only one. And as government becomes ever bigger and national politics ever more complex, that some-body has got to be, in many instances, a local.

For being what he is — and must be — he is neither con-demned nor looked down upon by more fortunate mem-bers of the House. He is, to the contrary, seen as a useful fellow if not, perhaps, the most stimulating of companions. And, as against another type, he is seen as a sound chap, indeed.

8

FREE RIDERS AND NATIONALS

THIS SECOND CHAP is the free rider, whose career in the House begins in accident, proceeds in disorder, and usually ends, by an act of predestination, fairly soon after it has begun. His annals are short but not simple and may be ten or a hundred times repeated in a single decade. He is the product of those (happily only occasional) convulsions of excessive national feeling — or, more properly, of irrational and extreme emotionalism — which will seize the people in hours of fear and frustration.

Dozens of his sort arrived in a Democratic Congress during the first four years of the Administration of Franklin D. Roosevelt, when this nation was in the cold grip of the Great Depression. It was a moment in history when the affrighted and totally perplexed voter was in a mood to turn upon all that was a part of, or even reminiscent of, that established order which, with a natural illogic, he supposed to be responsible for his current plight. Again, dozens of free riders arrived some ten years later, this time in a Republican Congress, the Eightieth.

Once more, the national mood was an aberration, this time a mood of weariness and cynicism and gross materialism. The death of Roosevelt as the Second World War drew to its close had left the people with a sense of rudderlessness. The accompanying and almost automatic and unthinking national denigration of his successor, Harry S Truman, was doing its work all too well. The people, moreover, suddenly became sick of the basic high-mindedness which had carried them through the war. Now they reached out for all they could get, under the great slogan of every man for himself. And in the concrete sense what they wanted most to get was more red meat; this was in the days of rationing and the point system. I recall traveling as a correspondent on President Truman's train to Missouri for the Congressional elections of that year, 1946. One of those aboard was Speaker Sam Rayburn. "How will the election go?" I asked him. "Easy to predict," he said, "it's going to be a God-damned beefsteak election. The ins are going out, my boy, and the outs are coming in."

And come in, indeed, they did; many and many of them, the Republican far-outs, as twelve and ten years before had come the Democratic far-outs. And as, very long before, the Radical Republican far-outs had come in, massively, at the close of the Civil War. The free riders who came from the elections of 1946 were superficially the antithesis of, but fundamentally the same as, those who had come in back in 1934 and 1936. Their terms of reference were different; but their basic motive was the same.

The earlier set of free riders abandoned all notion of personal thought or choice; they saw their mission as to vote with glad abandon for anything and everything which a Democratic President, Roosevelt, might offer to Congress. They did not bother overmuch even with looking after the affairs of their home districts. They made no contribution whatever to the business of the House beyond casting their votes with appropriate scorn for the pale cast of thought. And on some occasions they got beyond even the control of the hierarchy of the House. The leaders had followers all too eager to be led — anywhere — and thus were sometimes trampled upon from the rear.

Precisely the same things may be said of the Republican free riders of 1946, except that this time the medal's reverse side was turned to view. They, too, abandoned all notion of personal thought or personal choice. They, too, saw their mission as to vote with glad abandon *against* anything and everything which might be offered by a Democratic President. They, too, did not bother overmuch even with looking after the affairs of their home districts. They, too, made no contribution whatever to the business of the House beyond casting their votes with appropriate scorn for the pale cast of thought. And on some occasions they, too, got beyond even the control of the hierarchy of the House. The leaders had followers all too eager to be led — anywhere — and thus were sometimes trampled upon from the rear.

To recall some of the extraordinary men who swarmed over the House floor in the middle to late thirties and again in the middle to late forties is to recall scenes of surpassing strangeness, relative to the ordinary life of that place. . . . The shouting through, in the earlier time, of so-called bills which even the ever watchful leadership could not always either fully comprehend or fully defend. . . . The shouting through, a decade later, of uncomprehended measures designed not merely to embarrass but actually to cripple an American government in an hour full of all the complications and perils of a great war not yet wholly liquidated and of the dawning of an atomic era not yet faintly apprehended in all its infinite scope and meaning.

But though every House may have at least a few free riders, men who arrive with prefabricated convictions and never stay to hear the facts before handing in the verdict; and though some Houses will have a perilous many of them, the type is by its very nature an in-and-out, a transient type. Again, the odd factors that led to its odd elevation to office do not survive the inevitable clearing of atmosphere which will make that choice seem incredible in retrospect and irrelevant to present and future.

Moreover, there is always at hand yet another House type, who is ready and willing and able to sweep up the debris from the floor when the storm is passed, and who is, moreover, always at hand, even during the blow, to keep the damage to the lowest possible amount and the litter to the minimum. This is the House National, the member who, whether officially in high station or not, persistently occupies himself with national and world concerns to the last degree consonant with personal survival in a chamber which requires even the greatest of men never wholly to forget the small concerns of the people at home.

In the eighteen years or so during which I have had intimate knowledge of the House as it is inside as well as the House as it is outside, I have never known a time when the National type was not busily and usefully on the scene.

Sometimes, through circumstances of the kind just described, he may not be as useful as ideally he ought to be; but he never gives up. He is the sort of member who ought to have the ear and respect of the whole country, but never does; who ought to have medals for high public service under great difficulties, but never receives them; who ought, indeed, to be "promoted" to the Senate, but for the vital fact that he cannot be spared by the House — or spared from the House by the country either, if only the country knew.

The National spends all his days, and many of his nights, in a brilliant, intuitive, virtuoso performance of balancing off personal necessities, like that of bald political survival and the purely local good of his people at home, against national good. And the measure of his artistry and devotion is that most of the time he reaches a quite improbable and delicate, but nevertheless very real, poise on the scale of high service both to Congressional district and to Nation.

At this point in his work, he becomes an unrecognized national asset, an indispensable part of the public process — and, nearly every time, also a remarkably undemanding, and actually quite a selfless, man. It is he who makes the House worthwhile, who makes the House viable in a complex democracy; who gives to the House all that is good in it and, to the best of his very special ability, fends off from the House all that is bad in it. He is, so far as his attitudes would indicate, often just another fellow called Joe. And though his number is hardly legion, it is entirely true to the facts to call his number many. He engages the big and commits himself to largeness and the possible, while never scorning the small nor yet forgetting his obligations to the necessary.

9

SOME PERSONALITIES

FOR PURPOSES of illustration take a recent roster of the House for some characteristic examples, and look back into past rosters for others. There was the Democrat, Wilbur Mills of Arkansas, already mentioned in another connection. Mills, of course, was very high in the leadership, with all that this place implied in opportunity for decisive national service. But there was, at the same time, such a man as Walter Judd of Minnesota, a former medical missionary to China who, though occupying no elevated official position within the House, nevertheless for years was one of its special and informed consciences in foreign affairs from an area, the Middle West, which used to be thought of as "isolationist" and unconcerned with the troubles of peoples abroad.

Judd on many an occasion personally helped shape Far Eastern policy, to the degree that the House can really shape any foreign policy, on the basis of two qualifications and two alone: a capacity for endless work and study; and a long demonstration of the quality of informed disinterestedness on public matters. "Dr. Judd," as the House called him, may often have been wrong in his views. But he carried within himself a core of demonstrated personal and political integrity which raised up and commanded an unofficial following in the House, from an unofficial position as one of its elders and sages.

Again, there was Cleveland M. Bailey of West Virginia. He was not officially quite within the hierarchy of the House. But from his position on its Committee on Education and Labor this quiet, and nationally obscure, man was for many years one of the most powerfully influential voices in the nation on such matters as Federal aid to education, help for the sick and aged, and labor-management reform. How many, outside West Virginia, ever heard of Cleveland Bailey, even in connection with the issues here described? Yet it is a fact that Cleveland Bailey for at least a decade had more decisive influence in these fields than any one of a dozen Senators whose names spring readily to mind.

Or take such a truly submerged great national figure as George Mahon of Texas. Before he reached the top official leadership, Mahon for long years had a personal significance in the military affairs of this country hardly less real, if infinitely less known, than that of any of three successive Secretaries of Defense — Charles E. ("Engine Charlie") Wilson, Neil McElroy, Robert McNamara. A great, unspoken power had been exercised by this tall, quiet, graying Texan — whose face and name would be totally unknown to any conceivable national television audience — because of the great, inherent, bottom meaning of the House as the place where all home affairs are principally settled under that ultimate power over the public purse which is the ultimate power of the House.

Mahon (and there are in any Congress not a few Mahons)

is an unexcelled authority in military matters, wherever these matters are not wholly tactical and thus become the field of uniformed personnel. For, as chairman of an Appropriations subcommittee dealing with the military, long experience has told him where the money goes and how it flows and to what purposes in the vast labyrinth of the Pentagon. In these functions he is far more nearly a calm, coolly objective comptroller over the defense establishment than a "politician" in any sense in which that term is generally used.

Indeed, it is the Mahons — this particular George Mahon and others like him — who are the masters of that essentially dispassionate expertise by which the House performs nearly all its true *national* functions. A Mahon at work in the House is a thousand miles removed from any partisan political stump, from any noisy rally of the political faithful. He is part economist, part scientist, part military strategist in the high sense, that is, in the sense in which Congress may to a considerable degree predetermine future military strategy by the way in which it allots money to the Pentagon or withholds it. The doctrine of "massive retaliation" of the Eisenhower years, for an illustration, was an executive department creation in that it was proclaimed by Secretary of State John Foster Dulles, on the authority of the President, as the ultimate policy of this country. But "massive retaliation" would have been impossible either to adopt or to proclaim had not men like George Mahon been persuaded to permit it to develop by the way in which they channeled appropriations to the strategic bombardment arms of the Services on top of another vast outpouring of public money for the atomic weapons program.

Such defensive arrangements have their genesis in the minds and on the drawing boards of the military and diplomatic planners of this government. But they derive their sustenance, which is to say their life, in the small, cluttered and sometimes shockingly unimpressive offices of the George Mahons of the House. True, Senate offices have a not inconsiderable part in this progression from inception to reality; but they do not, most of the time, have the vital part. For, again, defense is by the deepest possible definition a home affair; and the House is the home of home affairs.

What is being discussed here is not, of course, the obvious circumstance that everything in the government, every plan and scheme, moves at last only upon the money granted by Congress. The point is not simply that Congress must provide the money; but rather that the wisdom or unwisdom of the way and scope in which the money is provided does not really rest in the end on the conscious decision of some large, generalized conceptual thing known as "Congress." In the end it rests upon the George Mahons — the Nationals who serve their country six days a week, and sometimes nights, and on the seventh do not rest but rather occupy themselves, on their day off, in looking after the local interests of local voters and the personal interest of being re-elected come the next relevant November.

For in the days before he became what he now is — the chairman of the entire Appropriations Committee — the generality of the House would ask, when the time came to act upon a military budget: "What does Appropriations say about this?" And the generality of the Appropriations Committee would ask: "What do our subcommittee fellows say about this?" And then the subcommittee itself would say to Mahon: "George, what do *you* say about this?"

Again, there is such a National as Thomas B. Curtis of Missouri. Curtis is that oddity, a free-enterprise Republican intellectual who, representing St. Louis County and South St. Louis, spends ten times as much effort in breaking the dreary codes of economic conundrums as he does upon the errands of his home folk. He does not and cannot neglect them; but like all the Nationals he does not hide from them his determination to serve as their Representative rather than as their messenger. Somehow he has arrived successfully at the thin balance between leading his people in the national essentials and allowing them to lead him in what really must be done for them locally. An authentically sound, gravely wry philosopher in and of Government, he is as valuable to the House, and to this country, as he is esteemed by the one and unremarked by the other.

And take two fairly recent Nationals — quite recent, indeed, as measured by the long slope of time on which the old Chamber rests, a man named John F. Kennedy and a man named Richard M. Nixon. Both later served in the Senate; and both later also served in yet more elevated places, Mr. Nixon as Vice President and Mr. Kennedy as President of the United States. When, in 1960, they met upon the campaign platforms of the country for the highest honor of all, the Presidency, it could be said of both that if their advanced political training had been obtained in the Other Body, their true political underpinnings had been hewn in the hard, unnoticing life of the House.

They had come there at the same time, to the Eightieth

Congress in 1946. And they were a pair of distinguished exceptions to the generally rather melancholy nature of the new selections made that year by the voters, in their wisdom, to the House of Representatives of the United States. For both, the House offered not so much opportunity to advance as opportunity to learn.

Kennedy learned the hard way, by throwing himself into the grinding routine of labor reform. This was the year that the Republicans brought on the Taft-Hartley Act; and there, very far down the table as a very junior member of the Labor Committee, Kennedy first discovered the vast distinction between slogans and reality, between ideologies and practicalities, in American politics.

He was, of course, a Democrat; and a Liberal Democrat, at that. In the ordinary way he was an automatically chosen follower of Big Labor, which at once set off a clamor that Taft-Hartley was a "slave labor" bill. But as he sat down there at the bottom of the table and heard the endless testimony, the unceasing flow and counterflow of fact and opinion, he found it at first difficult and then impossible to adopt so happily simple a view for his own. Gravely deferential to his party elders, perceptively quick to catch the realities of the hierarchial system of the House, he became a legislator, as distinguished from a hopeful young amateur not too long out of Harvard College, within the space of four months.

Kennedy thus involved himself in — or, in one of his favorite words, committed himself to — one of the hard, enduring domestic problems of this country. The House was not an easy place for him; there was a tendency among both Average and Above Average to refer to him with kindly and

unintended patronage as "that Kennedy boy from Massachusetts." He was incredibly youthful looking then. All the
same, he worked his own passage. And, more significant for
his future, there he learned that the heart of the effective
American political process lies in the compromises formed at
last by an *informed*, and not necessarily a mere numerically
superior, consensus. More than his later career in the Senate,
the House taught him the pains and pleasures of political
leadership; they were not his pains, not his pleasures; but he
caught their meaning from the elders and stored it up for
another day and another year.

Nixon as a National took a different route in the House; a
route which was in fact largely accidental. Circumstances
caused him to take a leading part in that excited search for
"communism-in-Government" which so preoccupied, and
often so bedeviled, this country in the late forties and early
fifties. The *quality* of his work in that period is not at issue
in this book; for the Great Red Hunt is many books in and
of itself, and to make judgment upon it would require a long
diversion from the task here in hand. The outcome of that
work, however, is profoundly relevant here. For its outcome
and its implications both thrust Nixon into a national prominence he might not otherwise have attained and long made
him politically vulnerable in that prominence.

For it was a work essentially alien to and in disharmony
with the kinds of work with which the House is properly at
home. Here were objectives which were not legislative and
essentially constructive, but rather investigative and essentially pejorative and punitive. The House is not made to be
an effective prosecuting agency though it does, indeed, have

the high, specialized prosecuting function under the Constitution of bringing bills of impeachment against public officials for trial by the Senate. The House is, most distinctly, not made to be a forum of justice, for justice is rightly an objective enterprise and the House is at bottom a great, swarming pit of men in which many subjectivities are flung one against the other with the ultimate aim of reaching some tolerable and rarely final and never perfect, accommodation of competing interests and conflicting desires.

10

MAKERS OF SYNTHESIS

THIS BLENDING of the desirable with the attainable, of the hundreds of clamoring local interests with the scores of sectional interests and the dozens of belligerently competitive national interests, could reasonably be described as both the ultimate purpose of the Nationals in the House and their reason for being. With the calm skill of good chemists who make a reasonably stable and viable synthesis of widely divergent elements which are mutually hostile in their raw and natural state, House Nationals at their best make a largely intuitive, and thus artistic, formula which will then be submitted to the more leisurely and delicate refining operations of the Other Body, the Senate.

Wherever the synthesis is really good, the Senate will seldom find it possible to reject it out of hand. It can often outargue the House; it can always outthink the House, if it really puts its mind to it. But it can never outwork the House. Nor can its best men outdo the best men of the House on the *facts* of a legislative measure, so long as these facts have been in the charge of the top level of the House Nationals.

These, the very elite among the elite who make up the Nationals, do not, of course, turn up every day or in every Congress. And it is a striking fact that most often when they do turn up they are more likely to be Democrats than Republicans. The circumstance, though unpalatable to the Republicans, is nevertheless recognized by the wiser among them as one of those odd facts of life, one of those japeries of fate. To give the probable reasons for its existence is necessarily an exercise in rather loose speculation.

My own view, after much observation and thought upon the matter, and expressed without partisan bent or motive, is that it arises from the very fact that Democrats, anywhere and everywhere, are generally both less disciplined and less cautious than Republicans, both institutionally and personally. This being so, they have more room for development in an essentially incautious — and sometimes also inchoate — chamber. And they undoubtedly move with fewer inhibitions. A man does not become an artist by conforming, not even by wisely conforming.

At all events, when this elite man among the elite who are the Nationals does inhabit the House, he stands astride it with a power (and indeed with a kind of grandeur) that is not found even among the ablest of the Senate types. His feet are not merely on the ground; they are on a ground — the ground of the House — upon which he is exquisitely and sensitively at home. He becomes a part of the place in the special sense that a great rider becomes a part of his horse; the impulse and capacity for the right action at the right time flow from one to the other like current over an unbroken circuit.

Such an elite National, years ago, was the aristocratic Republican Speaker, Nicholas Longworth of Ohio, who, because of what he was and not simply because of what position he held, became a power not only over the House but also within that Republican Party to which he gave only such interest and concern as he felt he could spare from the House.

Even more such a one, later on, was the determinedly man-of-the-people Democratic Speaker, Sam Rayburn of Texas. Rayburn, who had served longer as Speaker of the House than any man in history when he died in his seventy-ninth year, was by common definition the Man of the House, for this century at least. In his long life in the House as an elite National he had over a span of fifty years of service survived twenty-five consecutive Congressional elections from a district in Texas by finding it possible to represent its parochial interest at every turn without once allowing this parochial interest to injure his incomparably greater mission of helping to lead the United States of America in its highest policies, both domestic and foreign.

More than any other man in Congress in either House he was responsible for that part of the immense legislative program of the early Roosevelt New Deal that was both sound and enduring — the regulation of the stock exchanges, the breakup of the electric power holding companies' undue grasp on the economy, and indeed the whole complex of such of the Roosevelt economic reforms as would be able to pass the critical test of long-demonstrated usefulness to the Nation.

Along with this, he had, from the time of Woodrow Wilson

all through the years of Franklin Roosevelt and Harry Truman, stood as a great rock in the House in support of the movement of history which at long last turned this from an isolationist country to the leading and dominant force and voice of a world of internationalism. To this long and storied enterprise, this least selfish and most enlightened act of creation in foreign policy in the history of mankind, he had sometimes, indeed, been not only a supporter but actually a decisive contributor. It was Rayburn, going down into the Well of the House to make a memorable appeal on the eve of the Pearl Harbor disaster, who by a single vote saved the military draft from expiration in one of those reckless and puerile-minded moments which, on foreign affairs, will sometimes take the House by the throat like an epileptic seizure.

It was this square, bald, compactly stout, buttoned-up, laconic, and sometimes imperious Man of the House who upon a hundred great and now forgotten occasions, in a thousand crisis hours in the endless legislative story of this country, both personified and vindicated the best in the House. All Nationals must know the House well; this is the precondition of their state. He knew it intimately, understood it in an instinctual sense which surpasses understanding, bent it to his will, carried it on his back and dwelt with it in his blood and bones. It was, as he said in many private moments, his *life*, as it is actually the life of all the Nationals, though not perhaps in the profound and total way in which it was his.

He was a good politician by necessity, and by avocation, but a great legislator by vocation. Never in fifty years was his district in Texas other than behind him; never did he let it down but never did he let it run him or instruct his thinking.

It was deeply Conservative, small-farm, small-town, small-bank Conservative. He was anything but Conservative by its standards, and considerably less than Liberal by the standards of those Northern and Eastern ultra-Liberals — the Non-Average — with whom for decades he dealt in the House with a mixture of amused annoyance, exasperated affection, and tolerant hope. He sometimes referred to them in private as "those little boys," much like a parent contemplating, with both fond pride and contempt, the onset in a freshman son at college of those inevitable attitudes of rebellion which are healthy in the spirited young but tend to become only absurdly trying when they linger on.

In a word, Rayburn, with that immensely acute perception which comes to public men as rarely as the aching special skill of a Heifetz will come to a violinist, was able not only to sense readily the limitations of Non-Average in a House which will never really be their home. He was also able to understand — and usefully to exploit — the deep truth that Non-Average all the same has high uses in the House. Non-Average, if always a nuisance in any great current consensus in any House, is often also the messenger of tomorrow, the thinker of thoughts not quite apposite just now but one day to be apposite, indeed. Non-Average sometimes is a sand in the gears of the legislation of here-and-now which will produce in some long tomorrow a more relevant gear for what will then be more relevant legislation.

He was neither "Conservative" nor "Liberal," in the self-conscious and self-proclaimed sense. This was so because he knew that labels are nonsense, of a curiously uncertain coinage meaning many things to many men. And this was so because he knew his function was to act, to solve and to mediate — not to strike attitudes or to draw up those proud manifestos which are so rarely relevant to performance in the art of politics, of which art the House is, on the whole, a pretty good, if rather rough, studio and working place.

As the saying goes around that place, he could count the votes, as all Nationals can. And, as all Nationals do, he understood the limited value of the trappings, the slogans, the gear of politics. These are the implements of the game; the game itself is something else. The game is the act of governing; partisan politics is the tool in the hands of the governor. It is a part of the mechanics of power and performance; but it has within itself no special nobility. It is a thing and not a principle, a tactic and not a purpose.

Thus the Rayburns as the supreme expression of the National, and thus all the Nationals of the Congress now sitting and all the other Nationals of all the other Congresses that have ever sat, will at last concern themselves neither with sharply defined ideologies nor even with party labels. They will concern themselves with bringing consent and concert to the House, an enterprise in which the sheep of one day may be the goats of another. Thus they do not madly try to divide the sheep from the goats, except on unimportant occasions, or on occasions where appeals to such simplifications seem the only likely way to get done what they wish to be done.

For the true tale of the House at work would never make a spirited television drama, nor does it well accord with those breathless confrontations of the good guy against the bad guy which the partisan committees of both political parties regularly offer the voting public in every Congressional election year. The theory of mechanical politics, which is to say of the political committees, is that of a simple tableau in which, given more Republican seats (or Democratic seats), all will be well with Republican (or Democratic) purposes. The actuality of House politics is that action on great issues generally comes down the center of the House, through momentary mergers of the centers of both parties which will perhaps fly apart on another question tomorrow and then come together again on yet another question in some not distant day-after-tomorrow.

In these moments the party identification of the National at work at the middle of this movement will not be insignif-icant; if he is a member of the majority party he will, of course, have a greater hand than the minority party National in setting the course, the tone and the duration of the strug-gle. All the same, this identification will not be decisive. For in legislative moments of truth the minority party National and the majority party National will very often be working only nominally at cross-purposes and actually to the same purpose. This purpose, of which Rayburn was perhaps the most brilliant of all expositors, is the high one of keeping both Majority and Minority on responsible paths; to make the contest run with spirit but also with due regard for the rights of advocates and dissidents alike. For, to repeat, the dissident of today may become the indispensable ally of tomorrow, and vice versa. The ultimate and inescapable obligation of the Nationals is to keep hysteria at bay in the whole House, in rare times of extraordinary passions, and to keep manifest unfairness, to men or to issues, away from any part of the House in the quite ordinary and usual times when men fighting over a bill may not scruple too much about the means to their ends.

A certain military analogy comes to mind. The National lacks nothing whatever in the way of determination to win the legislative engagement to which he has committed himself. But, like a good officer of Infantry, it is his duty to look beyond the immediate objective to see to it that his own men so conduct themselves as not to invite undue and unnecessary reprisals in the actions yet to come and to see to it also that his own casualties are not excessively high in the action immediately at hand, as measured by its degree of importance in the larger design of the larger battle.

11

THE SPEAKER

IN A SENSE, therefore, the Nationals are bound together, above and beyond party, so that they form the mind and heart of the House. They are members of Congress far more than they are members of parties; it is not uncommon to see one of them give stealthy help to another in an election year of a kind which, looked at in a superficial light, would seem remarkably like trading with the partisan enemy.

To the House itself such help, such amenities, so to speak, within the lodge, are quite common and open. For years Sam Rayburn and Joseph W. Martin, Jr., of Massachusetts alternated in an amiable game of musical chairs. Whenever the House went Democratic, Rayburn stepped up from his old position as minority leader to the Speakership. Martin climbed down from the dais to take up his new position as minority leader for the Republicans down on the floor. Then the whole process was reversed, when the election returns put the Republicans back in control.

Each exchange of place was accompanied by a grave and genuinely meant exchange of civilities, in spirit not unlike

that between Grant and Lee at Appomattox, and with that
light partisan banter which is a part of the game. "You take it
now, Joe," Rayburn would say to Martin, "but I'll be back
on this dais after the next election." "You take it now, Sam,"
Martin would say, "but I'll be back on this dais after the next
election."

When the Speakership changes hands, many perquisites,
large and small, change, too. One of these, of the small variety, is the right to occupy a series of offices in which the
Speaker conducts his multifarious activities. One of these is
a jewellike retreat, paneled in mahogany and beautiful
with age, which is a secondary Speakership suite some dis-
tance from the distractions of the floor of the House. Near to
it is a much smaller, and far less elegant, suite for the minority leader.

When, in 1955, he made one of his periodic returns to
power, Rayburn was, of course, in this smaller office. He
looked about him, sighed at the imminent task of moving all
his personal things once again, and telephoned to Martin.
"Joe," he said, "to hell with all this nonsense. You keep the
big office." This Martin did. It is not of itself a significant
anecdote, except for this: tradition is a big thing in the
House (if far less than in the Senate, which lives and breathes
tradition) and big, too, are its symbols and trappings. Rayburn, for the first time in the history of the House, was in so
explicit a way recognizing a brotherhood of the Nationals
which transcends, though never quite destroys, party lines,
even though party lines determine the ultimate housekeeping control of the House.

In short, the power of the Nationals, though real, is pressed into relatively compact areas. Fully expressed in the laws of this country, this power does not necessarily express national aspirations generally or even the aspirations of the national political parties generally. Joseph Martin, the perennial Republican Speaker for a very long time, and Sam Rayburn, the perennial Democratic Speaker for a far longer time, had great moral influence over their respective parties. But they had little of the real and decisive power, as distinguished from prestige, within those parties which was held by Governors and even, though more rarely, by United States Senators.

The basic constituency of the official often called "the second most powerful man in the United States," the Speaker of the House, is, after all, not the national forum of the House but rather the comparatively poky little Congressional district from which, perforce, he comes.

To the political parties, even the most notable Speaker is still only a member of Congress, whereas even a pretty dim sort of Governor is still a Governor, and even a pretty dim sort of Senator is still a Senator with mandates, however shaky, running the length and breadth of a whole state with a number of electoral votes. Rayburn in his greatest hours had the largest influence over his party of any Speaker in history. All the same, it was a very relative thing. He was, for illustration, never nearly as influential at a national party convention as was his protégé and unofficial "son," Lyndon B. Johnson, from the instant Johnson reached the United States Senate.

"Mr. Democrat" he was for many a Democratic convention; and of many of them he was Permanent Chairman. But his effective and operative power in these affairs was always more shadowy than real; more a matter of symbolism than of pragmatic fact. Morally, he might, and did, tower above the several enclaves of harsh and struggling power and counter-power which any convention will produce wherever there is a genuine choice of alternatives for a Presidential nomination. Practically speaking, however, he was both above and below them in terms of critical influence. Above them in that he was incomparably more important to the party's *legislative* plans than all of them put together; below them in the far more vital sense that collectively they knew where the votes were for the nomination of a President, and collectively could deliver these votes.

The political life of the House, as to a lesser extent of the Senate, is a life of comparatively high expertise which, at the last, means dealing with issues more than with men, with abstractions more than with the naked search for personal power. These are the politicians of the performing arts of government. The others — the convention politicians — are the politicians who promise, who create the blocs of raw power, in the shape of delegate votes, upon which will be chosen a man who, as President, will then enter into a performing relationship with the House.

A national political convention is thus twice an unreal forum for the House National: always he is in the wrong place for his talents; and often he is doing the wrong, or ineffective, thing in that place. However full of honors and renown, he can offer to the common partisan enterprise of defeating the other party's Presidential nominee not divisions or even regiments of troops, but at best only companies or platoons.

Old "Cactus Jack" Garner, a tough and effective Speaker of the House, was not merely kicked upstairs when, in 1932, he was chosen to be Vice President on the ticket with Franklin D. Roosevelt. He was, from that moment onward, in the wrong place and attempting to do the wrong thing in his efforts to abate what he thought to be the excessive liberalism of the first Roosevelt New Deal. Still on the high dais in the House he could, perhaps, have brought the New Deal more nearly to his own wishes when the time came for its legislative implementation. But, held as he was in the Administration's genteel captivity as Vice President, he could only look on and mutter; his power was gone. Once, one of his old conservative Texas friends, John Henry Kirby, wrote Vice President Garner in alarm about what he considered to be the unwise and unexampled interventions of the President's wife, Eleanor Roosevelt, into politics of all kinds, including internal Democratic politics. Kirby suggested that Garner forthwith demand of Roosevelt that he "do something about Mrs. R."

Garner, a notably laconic man as are many of the true House Nationals, replied in a letter eloquent of his powerlessness in the matter — and also of the wry ability of a good House man to jerk his vis-à-vis around from an offensive to a defensive position in the space of a moment. "Dear John Henry," he wrote, "I have your letter. How long has it been since *you* have controlled *your* wife? Yours, John."

Again, to illustrate the fact that the Speakership is immense in government but much less than that in partisan politics, there was the more recent episode of 1962 in which the nephew of Speaker John W. McCormack, Eddie McCormack, was running for the Democratic nomination for the Senate against the youngest brother of the President, Teddy Kennedy. Many billed this in advance as a titantic and fateful clash of two Democratic "dynasties" in Massachusetts. To the degree that this suggested a collision of roughly equal forces, the billing was the most puerile of nonsense. John Mc-Cormack's real writ in Massashusetts, like Rayburn's in Texas and like Joseph Martin's in Massachusetts, ran over a Congressional District, and nothing more. John McCormack's power in the Congress of the United States was, and would remain, so far above that of young Teddy Kennedy as to make comparison ridiculous. But John McCormack's power in Massachusetts was another thing altogether.

Sam Rayburn's memory will live long in history, and forever in the memory of the House of Representatives of the United States. But this man who had the capacity to help alter the course of the Republic in some of its most urgent years and hours could, I think, never have been elected to statewide office in his own state. He held a long, shy and unspoken dream for the Presidency of his country, an honest dream because of his attainments. But it was the wrong dream for him. It was wrong because his place was the wrong place from which to hope to reach the dream, and because the very qualities which made him a matchless leader in what was for him the right place, the House, were not the qualities which could open that other place to him.

The topmost House National is a great man; and often also a good man. But he is a man of *some* of the people — those, that is, who people the House and are in fact far more discriminating and difficult to please than the run of the public. But he is never a man of *all* the people. And never in all history has a topmost House National reached the Presidency, save for James Madison himself.

III

THE CENTERS
AND USES
OF POWER

12

THE COMMITTEES

THE House of Representatives as a collective thing might well be described as a large number of men foregathering in a great hall, the House chamber, in reasonable amity and usefulness merely to set seal upon the final details of high business already settled in principle for it by a series of tough-minded, able and dutiful agents who know what the House and country need and want, far better than does the corporate House itself.

These agents form, and are, the centers of both power and decision. And, though highly human, indeed, they are called, by a formidably awkward and unhuman title, Standing Committees. It is a term which connotes a dustiness, a fustiness, and perhaps a kind of archaic confusion of procedure and purpose which is in no possible way applicable to the facts of the case.

The present House of Representatives is made up of twenty such Standing Committees, of which none is wholly without mandate over some part of the life of this country and of which at least seventeen reach deeply and intimately into our affairs. There is Agriculture, which, of course, helps decide how much fiber and food are to be grown and where, and under what Federal restrictions and Federal bounties. There is Appropriations, which, as the saying goes, needs no introduction; it allocates the money for Federal expenditures and, in the process, carries on an endless war of perquisite and prestige with the companion Standing Committee in the Other Body.

There is Armed Services, which largely decides such poignant matters as how soon Johnny is to be drafted and how many Johnnies are to be called and when; how much money should be recommended for missiles or mortars; what high strategic stance this country should take in the eternal warfare between the claims of conventional and nuclear force. There is Banking and Currency (a deceptive term, this one), which goes far beyond the regulation of banks and currency to handle such household intimacies as price controls and such national intimacies as economic mobilization. There is Education and Labor, which supervises all labor-management legislation, puts forward or denies any and all forms of Federal aid to education, and otherwise runs the dizzying gamut of welfarism, pensions, unemployment insurance, medical care and so on, from slightly beyond the cradle to slightly short of the grave.

There is Foreign Affairs, which officially has a large measure of control over foreign policy, including such venerable perennials as foreign aid and such occasional papers of state as resolutions backing an American President in, say, a crisis in the Chinese offshore islands, in Berlin or in Cuba or Southeast Asia. To say that Foreign Affairs is as truly powerful in

its field as are the other major Standing Committees is to
overstate, for reasons to which I shall return. For the moment,
however, and for listing purposes, it must be granted its place
in this catalogue.

There is Government Operations, which keeps a skeptical
and roving eye of concern over the functioning of the Executive Department of this government, from the White House
down, and from whose labors and watchings can come much
grief upon occasion to the bureaucrats "downtown." (Washington, for governmental purposes, is in two parts. "Downtown" is The Administration; "The Hill" is Congress. The
great marble palace of the Supreme Court of the United
States sits, too, upon Capitol Hill, frowning ever so slightly
and with a certain portentousness across a leafy plaza at the
House and Senate. But, in the habit of the city, and indeed
also of the Government, the Supreme Court is on but not of
Capitol Hill.)

There is Interior and Insular Affairs, which handles legislation dealing with national parks and monuments, grazing
lands in the West, and many kinds and shapes of conserva-
tion programs. To the far Westerner, Interior is a kind of
distant mixture of Heaven and Hell; from it flow many large
blessings, but also, sometimes, harsh ukases and interdictions
which may be hard to understand and accept in Wyoming,
in Colorado, in Arizona, in New Mexico, in Montana and
the like. There is Interstate and Foreign Commerce, which
regulates the buses, the railroads, the airlines, television and
radio, stock markets, power companies and such other enterprises.

There is Judiciary, which, with a truly vast mandate, oversees Federal courts and prosecutors, accepts or rejects bills on civil rights, proposes or denies Constitutional amendments, and is, naturally, brimful of lawyers in a House which is by no means short of them everywhere. There is Post Office and Civil Service, which raises or lowers mail rates, pays the postmen, and looks after the teeming and faceless swarm of government men and women who work down more or less in the bowels of the most giant bureaucracy in the world. There is Public Works, which says yea or nay to the great dams, the power projects and so on with which the country is increasingly dotted. There is storied Rules, which largely controls the flow or nonflow of bills to the floor of the House. (Of this much, much later.)

There is Science and Astronautics, which sits over the American space program, the Cape Kennedys and all the rest. There is Un-American Activities, whose work, for ill or for good, is known to every schoolboy. There is Veterans Affairs, which looks after the interests of veterans. And finally, there is Ways and Means, which handles tariffs, taxes, and, in a sense, more or less everything.

The first House, which met in New York City in the spring of 1789, put its main reliance on the whole House and had only one Standing Committee — that on Elections — whose function it was to make sure that the men appearing there had, indeed, been lawfully and properly elected. The early custom was to hand over a bill or a problem to a special, *ad hoc* committee to go off and ponder the matter and return with its proposals. In the nineteenth century, however, it became plainly necessary to establish Standing Committees, meaning committees of fixed and permanent jurisdiction to work consecutively at the matters assigned to them. And so for more than a century now these have been the centers of a power whose uses have at once made possible the work of the House and raised up within it a structure of creation and command.

This inner structure is in the real and true sense more decisive than is the outer House. It is a paradoxical case (and all politics in fact is expressed in a series of paradoxes) in which the smaller inside of the House is bigger than the larger outside which is the whole House.

Senior membership in an important House committee, let alone chairmanship of such a committee, involves a grant to the recipient of an institutional power and prestige which is found in no other legislative body on earth. It is not quite found in the United States Senate, where the cult of personality cuts across the cult of committee. Certainly it is not found in the British House of Commons, where no committee can be independent, in the end, of the party instrumentality which finally makes all major decisions.

This senior membership is, true enough, reached by way of seniority in the House, by the simple capacity to survive a lengthening series of elections at home. But a member must first of all be started upon the long road. And in order even to start upon the road that may lead at last to real seniority, he must first pass the acid test of being acceptable, at the beginning, to yet another aspect of the committee system.

13

MEN OF INFLUENCE

EVERY new Congress brings new members and every new Congress involves a dignified but urgent scramble among the new to be assigned to some committee of true significance.

Every new member of the House must owe his beginnings to the elders who have sat there long before him. If he is a Democrat, he must look to the Ways and Means Committee, which on its Democratic side, for this single purpose of filling committee assignments momentarily calls itself the Committee on Committees. When the Democrats are in control of the House itself, and thus of the Ways and Means Committee, the Democratic side of Ways and Means, functioning as the Committee on Committees, determines to which committee — major or minor — each new Democratic member shall go. Each member of Ways and Means is allocated a geographic zone from within which he may make nominations. Such nominations are at length carried to the Democratic caucus of the House — and there adopted.

Ways and Means thus is the dictator of committee assign-

ments on the Democratic side of the House. But this exclusive
power it does not, as a matter of practice and common
sense, press too far. After all, the Speaker of the House, though
not himself a member of Ways and Means, or of any other
committee, has an enormous influence there. A word from
him to the chairman, or to one or more of the senior members,
in behalf of so and so, will rarely fail to accomplish its purpose. If he is a "strong" Speaker, his suggestion will have a
touch of the royal command; in the nature of things his association with Ways and Means is both close and cordial. Very
often, his influence may well have been decisive in placing
upon Ways and Means this member who is now its chairman or one of its ranking members. Moreover, if Ways and
Means ever consistently refused a Speaker's advice in so intimate a matter as a committee assignment, a fundamental
crisis would be at hand.

Either Ways and Means, under its momentary hat as the
Committee on Committees, would on second thought wisely
become more amenable, or the Democratic caucus of the
whole House might override Ways and Means, under its
momentary hat as the Committee on Committees, to uphold
the ultimate moral authority of the Speaker. One solution
or the other would paralyze the House of Representatives,
and thus Congress and the Government itself. Such things
don't happen here, for the simple reason that supernally foolish men simply do not arrive at the chairmanship of Ways
and Means or the Speakership of the House.

On the Republican side, the comparable Committee on
Committees is made up, not of the Republican members of
Ways and Means but rather of a special group of elders com-

posed of the senior Republicans in the House from each of the fifty States.

The distinction is not, however, great in practice, for in the natural order of things *some* of the senior Republicans will in any event also be members of Ways and Means, and *all* of them will be under the influence of Ways and Means.

Thus, while the committee system is the heart of the House, the heart of the committee system lies in Ways and Means. As *the* big Committee of the House, Ways and Means has two rivals — Appropriations and Rules. Appropriations has, theoretically, the power to force Ways and Means to its knees — by withholding appropriations from regions or bills favored by unfavored members of Ways and Means. Rules has, theoretically, the power to apply pressure on Ways and Means, because Rules, to a point, has the power, as the traffic regulator of the House, to prevent bills — except these originating in Ways and Means — from coming to the floor for action. This, again in theory, could deny clearance to certain bills specially favored by unfavored individual members of Ways and Means.

Again, however, this is not the sort of thing that happens in practice. For in its classic and unique grasp on the very makeup of all other House committees, Ways and Means also has this grip on the makeup of Appropriations and Rules. Conceivably, Ways and Means could come in, at the onset of some new Congress, with an entirely new slate of assignees to both Appropriations and Rules. Practically speaking, it would never do so. And, speaking for a certainty, neither the Speaker nor the whole House would ever permit it to do so.

Thus, in actuality Ways and Means, Appropriations and

Rules coexist, not merely in the mundane spirit of live and let live but in the higher spirit of a shared awareness that together they are both the leaders and the exemplars of the House. In this they are subject always to some extent to the wishes of the Speaker, who sits as a kind of monarch over all, and nearly always to some extent to the wishes of the party leaders, who are more or less ministers to the crown.

There are, however, party leaders and party leaders, as there are also Speakers and Speakers. No party leader is ever ignored; and no Speaker is every wholly unfeared. But some party leaders are more gladly heeded than some others — as, to take current examples, is Charles Halleck of Indiana for the Republicans. And some Speakers are more instantly respected, down to the last detail, than others — as, to take past examples, were Sam Rayburn of Texas, John Garner of Texas and William Bankhead of Alabama.

For the ultimate truth of it all is that decisive influence in the House depends 20 percent on position due to seniority — a not inconsiderable 20 percent — and 80 percent on the complex matter of who the man of influence *is*. This is to say that no committee chairman or the like, even granting that he is personally weak or even personally obnoxious, is anything like powerless. He is very far from that. But it is also to say that those who reach the very acme of power must have much more to offer than mere possession of defined and hierarchial spheres of influence within the committee and seniority structure.

While it is practically impossible to remove a committee chairman, it is by no means impossible to reduce his operating influence — so long as the job is done with a certain quiet taste and in ways not ever making it clear that it is being done at all. There have been many instances, some few of which have been seen at close range by this writer, where the supposedly sacrosanct protection of seniority has been allowed to remain more a shadow than a substance. R. Ewing Thomason, later a Federal judge in Texas, was for a critical time in the early postwar period the real chairman of the old House Committee on Military Affairs (before its merger into the Committee on Armed Services). The titular chairman was one Andrew May of Kentucky, an amiable bumbler who also, unhappily for him, later got into trouble with the Federal authorities on a matter relating to influence peddling. This transfer of actual command, of which the whole House knew everything, but of which the whole House never whispered a syllable outside the institution, was done without frontal challenge to the system; and with never a word of it being said by anybody in authority.

Again, to take a much more recent example, there is the case of Representative Adam Clayton Powell of Harlem, New York. Powell's lighthearted tendencies in 1963 to take expensive trips to Europe on government funds (in which some continental nightclubbing was involved) and to absent himself from some of his urgent House duties produced no "Powell-must-go" chant in the House.

What it did produce, however, was a decision among the other hierarchs of the House to begin to cut him down to size by the homely but effective means of sharply reducing the budget allowed by the House for his work as chairman of the Committee on Labor. If Powell had, indeed, been too much at play, it was so arranged that in future, House displeasure would be felt in this most intimately practical way. Does this seem not very effective? It will be well to wait and see.

If a Supreme Court justice removable only by an impeachment process of incomparable difficulty and of all but intolerable messiness and shock to the American system goes wholly inept at his work it does not follow that the system of ultra-seniority which appointed him for life is itself wrong. I strongly suspect that if such a case should ever arise, his brethren on the high bench would make arrangements to shift the main burden of his work elsewhere and let the thing go at that.

At any rate, the House has never abandoned and will not, I think, ever abandon the seniority system. But it will take measures not to permit a bad example of that system to do consistent and measurable harm to the public interest. It was done in the May case simply by seeing to it that Thomason really spoke for the committee, while May kept all the perquisites except that of actual leadership.

14

SENIORITY

"SENIORITY" is one of the most complex and difficult aspects of the whole life of the House, and the one most often and most bitterly under attack in recent years. Granted the inherent power held by even the least of committee chairmen, it is argued, how can it be justified that this enormous position should be reached simply through the circumstance of political longevity? There are good reasons, though they require a deal of telling. But perhaps the best reason of all is that there is, the more one knows the House, simply no viable alternative. The easy solution offered is to have the members of each committee elect their own chairman. But the notion is far too attractively simple.

In the first place, this process, though easy of description, would be immensely complicated and dangerous in practice. What it would amount to would be a system of choice based either upon a kind of Gallup poll or upon a series of log-rolling and vote-catching techniques: you give me a vote here and I will give you a vote on that bill of yours, and so on. The resultant infighting, particularly as to committees dealing intimately with the harsher and more emotional national issues, would produce a lobbying chaos in the House in which "outside" pressures, not all of them necessarily beneficent and forward-looking and disinterested, could simply tear the place apart.

Nor could there possibly be any objective standard upon which objective men could rely. Is such and such a committee chairman only a fossil and fuddy-duddy — or is he a very wise old man who has seen much and many come and go in the House and is thus armed with the unique value of long experience? Is the test here to be one's ideology — and if so what ideology should be controlling, the conservative, the liberal, the moderate, the merely pragmatic? Moreover, what is to be said for the factor of long awareness of the special problems which this committee must endlessly and over and over confront? Is it better to have as chairman the man who knows it all backwards and forwards, even if one disagrees on ideology with him, or to have as chairman a man with whom one wholly agrees but who has had no time or opportunity to learn of the entangled issues which are, and must be, this committee's unceasing writ and task?

Beyond the slightest doubt, the House itself prefers the former kind of chairman to the latter. On the basis of simple observation, moreover, individual members, even those who come to the House determined to end what they believe to be a system of iniquity, believe in the seniority system the more strongly the longer they remain in the House. This, of course, is in part due to the obvious fact that the longer they stay the higher they themselves have climbed upon seniority's ladder. All the same, this is not the controlling or even the principal reason for this devotion to the system. It survives primarily because the more it is examined, for all its undoubted faults, the more viable it is seen to be in terms of the practical experience of the men of the House, not excluding the most reformist-minded of them.

Over and over again, the hot-eyed rebel from the committee system becomes, as intractable reality works its way with him, its stanchest defender. Again, one must return to the great, root truth that the House is a place where performance is the one true test; where means must in every case submit themselves to ends; where Condition meets Theory and in every case triumphs.

National political conventions come and go. And every national political convention, and most particularly every Democratic convention, has, as a part of the struggles that go on before its platform-writing committees, an old and endless tableau: those who wish to reform Congress return again and again to argue against the seniority system. They point to its seeming inequity; they point to individual House committee chairmen who are elderly or crochety or notoriously of a single ideological view — almost always the conservative point of view.

In the nature of things those who so point are almost always themselves of liberal persuasion and liberal origin — from organized labor, from minority group interests, and so on. What they say is appealing on its face. But each political convention has heard it all before; and each political convention will always make sure that the membership of its platform committee will include members of the House.

These weary worthies will perforce listen in patience,

and, for that matter, usually with a good deal of sympathy which will not for a moment alter their conviction that seniority must nevertheless stay in the House. They will applaud the sincerity of the protesting forces; hour upon hour they will listen to all the reasons why seniority must go. In the end, however, they will see to it that the platform makes no effective demand for its abolition; this is their ultimate duty to the House and to simple realism.

In the 1956 Democratic national convention which renominated Adlai E. Stevenson for President, it was my task to report the proceedings of the platform committee. During one very long day nearly the whole of the hearing was devoted to complaints about the seniority system. When it was at last all over, one of the platform writers, John W. McCormack, the present Speaker of the House, leaned back in fatigue, placed his arm around a Negro colleague on the platform committee, Representative William Dawson of Illinois, and addressed the witnesses who had so long been addressing him.

He said to them in substance that he undesrtood and respected their position but that there was, inside the House and inside the realities as distinguished from the theories, an actuality of experience that *they* did not understand. And then, proceeding from these generalities, he capped his counterargument with a single master stroke directed to the last of the complaining witnesses, the spokesman for a Negro organization. "You see," said McCormack, with his arm close around Dawson, "if it were not for the seniority system in the House I am bound to tell you that I very much doubt that my friend Bill Dawson would be today the chairman of a

House committee." The point was that Dawson would not have been chosen as chairman in a free election of the members.

What can be said of the rights and wrongs of the seniority system can be said to a point, but only to a point, of the famous Rules Committee, which is widely represented, and sometimes in part correctly, as a device to deny the majority's will by "bottling up" bills through denying them "a rule," meaning a clearance, to the House floor.

By one of the many ironies and paradoxes which are in the history of the House, the very power of this committee, a quite undue power in some instances, was granted to it by an insurgent movement of 1910 which had precisely the opposite aim. The Speakership then had been developed to the point where its current occupant, old "Czar" Joe Cannon, was appointing all members of House standing committees and was himself chairman of the Committee on Rules.

The long and short of this was that Speaker Cannon not only held every committee in the House in his *personal* grip; he was also *personally* able to decide, in practice alone, which bills should be brought to the floor and which not. A revolution led by the maverick Republican George Norris of Nebraska (later a famous Senator) stripped Cannon of his authority to appoint House committees and deliberately increased the corporate power of the Rules Committee.

The job, as it has since turned out, was all too well done from the viewpoint of the reformers. The reform which was intended to strike arbitrary power from the hands of the Speaker has, to a very large extent, only transferred that power to the Committee on Rules. Ideally, and theoretically, this committee should be a mere instrument of the

Speaker, bearing in mind that its assigned function is not to legislate or to pass upon legislation but only to serve as a housekeeping, traffic-regulating arm of the dominant House party leadership. In practice, however, Rules has become far more than this — though, again, not nearly so much more as many critics believe.

For Rules is not and never will be wholly independent of any strong-willed Speaker — as Sam Rayburn proved in 1961 by forcing some modification of its power, if, admittedly, not enough from some viewpoints.

Nor is it, even granting to it the somewhat excessive power imputed to it by its harshest critics, actually able to defeat the majority will of the House *if that majority is really determined upon its course.* A simple majority of the House can always bypass the Rules Committee by adopting a motion to "discharge" it from any bill upon which it may be sitting overlong.

The real trouble here is twofold. In the first place, Rules for years has been largely in the hands of conservative Republicans and conservative Democrats. What is wrong with the committee would be right with the committee, in the minds of its more liberal critics, if the coalition was composed of Liberals rather than Conservatives. And in the second place, there has not thus far been in modern times *any* genuine resolution on the part of the House generally to cut Rules down very much.

The reasons are these: Rules is not merely an obstructive device; it is also a protective device for many and many a member of the House, in every session. Say he is being pressed at home to vote for a bill which is clearly within his constituents' desire but which in heart and conviction he

really does not favor. So long as Rules does not clear it for
the floor, he has the best of all possible excuses to his constituency — he wants the bill but that committee won't let
him have it.

The truth therefore is that if Rules did not exist it would
have to be invented in some form at least. There must be,
somewhere in the House, some agency with the will or the
mere obstinacy, depending upon one's point of view toward
a particular bill, to keep it inert. Many members who cry out
in public at this little group of willful men, to paraphrase a
protest made by Woodrow Wilson against the Senate fili-
busters of his era, privately thank heaven that this little
group is around to sink an issue into prolonged limbo.

But for the Rules Committee we should have on our books
a good many more foolishly repressive measures — against
"aliens," against alleged "subversives" and hell-raisers in
general as measured by the irrationally high fears of dissent
and of mere cussedness that sometimes afflict our society in
hours of real or presumed foreign peril — than we have now.

Indeed, I am prepared to assert that all the "good" bills
more or less "killed" by the Rules Committee over all the
years would not, on any calm and rational scale of judgment,
outweigh all the crackpot measures, products of the momentary hysterias which infallibly and cyclically fall upon us,
which have been quietly put into limbo by it.

The fact is that the generality of the House sometimes will
not itself stand up against notably bad legislation given a
national climate whipped up by emotion, which is "demanding" that legislation. At such times, the generality of the
House needs a buffer, a protector. It is one thing for a member to go home and say he did not vote for some monstrous

foolishness "because it didn't come up." It is quite another thing to have to stand up and be counted, for or against.

For one illustration, it is a commonly accepted and quite non-partisan and non-ideological truism among able politicians that no member of the House from a "swing," or historically marginal, district can afford within a single session of Congress to go to bat publicly on more than three truly controversial issues. This is as true of a "good" member as of a "bad"; it is simply a fact of political life.

Now this should not be read as unduly cynical, unless one has an irrationally starry-eyed view of all mankind. Members of Congress are also men. The best of them do not gladly rush out always and on every occasion to court suicide by voting against a bill they believe to be bad. Nor do they relish the opportunity to vote for such a bill, standing for the principle that constituents are always right and meanly sinking personal principle. Whenever such a dilemma occurs — and its occurrence is rare, as the Rules Committee's "bottling up" process is also rare — there must be a way out as between two surrenders, the one of political life itself and the other of personal principle. There is in House politics, as indeed in all politics, an unuttered standard which I once called the limits of permissible demagoguery. Ideally, no doubt, no chemical trace of demagoguery is permissible. But politics persistently and inevitably apes life, and in all life, in all its forms, there is some element of demagoguery. All men bend to *some* extent to external pressures if only to make the small compromises of ordinary civility. If they do not they cease to be functioning men in the society in which they live.

15

"RULES"

THE GREAT THING in the House is to hold one's demagoguery to the lowest possible level. But a certain demagoguery — and I deliberately use an overly harsh term to illustrate the position here — is sometimes necessary to maintain the greatest careers in the highest of the public interest. To the old aphorism that a statesman is a politician who is dead, the House adds another aphorism of its own: To be a statesman a man must first be elected — and, in the case of the House, re-elected and re-elected again and again.

Proud manifestos of total and unqualified political "independence" are fine for slogans; but no good man in all the history of American politics, from Abraham Lincoln and before him down to today, has ever been utterly and eternally free of those compromises which are a part of political life — and which, indeed, *are* political life.

The truth of the business is that the House Rules Committee serves more or less the function of the Senate filibuster.

No Senate filibuster in history has ever prevented a truly devoted and determined Senate majority from having its will on *any* bill. Just so, no House Rules Committee in history has ever prevented a truly devoted and determined House majority from having *its* way on any bill whatever. Those who insist otherwise are driven by partisan or ideological zeal to overlook the enormous distinction between true and ostensible majorities. A dozen bills with the support of ostensible majorities may die in a single House session; when they do, the ostensible majority is not a real one.

An excellent argument, therefore, can be made that the Rules Committee is altogether too powerful and should be restrained to make passage of hotly disputed measures *easier*. Just so, an excellent argument can be made that the total destruction of the Senate right of filibuster would make easier the passage there of hotly disputed bills, say those on civil rights. It is not true, however, to say that any rule, any existing procedure, in either House actually *prevents* action on any measure supported with determination by a true majority, as witness the passage of the Civil Rights bill in 1964.

Reform may proceed notwithstanding this bedrock reality; and perhaps it should for that matter, at least as to the Rules Committee. But reform will not proceed in candor and realism until it is admitted that what is really sought is not the breaching of unbreachable barriers which do not in fact exist, but only the breaking of difficult barriers which already can in fact be breached. Not a dozen members of the House would deny this in the safety of absolute privacy. The long dialogue about Rules Committee reform thus proceeds upon stated principles which may be sound but upon premises of fact which are anything but sound.

But whether the principles themselves are wholly sound is itself debatable. For obstructive procedures in the House, like the filibuster in the Senate, are at bottom an expression of an American political instinct which to a point at least is one of great genius. This instinct is to fear and to try to delay or denature the sharpest of those sudden public impulses or passions which sometimes sweep the whole nation much as an unheralded hurricane may strike the American coastline.

The business of the House is, after all, to initiate and to legislate, and public demands for this or that action are not always wise simply because they are widespread and urgent. The process of delaying and denaturing is good, not bad, so long as it is not carried to the point of ultimate denial of what a properly informed and nonhysterical public wants to be done.

When, some years ago, President Harry S Truman recalled General of the Army Douglas MacArthur from his command in the Far East, the General was invited to address a joint session of both Houses of Congress sitting together in the House chamber. His speech, in which he declared that old soldiers never die but only fade away, caught the country in an emotional storm. We were involved in a terrible and seemingly hopeless war in Korea; MacArthur's rejected policies had seemed attractive in their simplicity. "Victory" was what he demanded. But some knew what the public at the moment seemed not to know. The issue was not whether General MacArthur's military policies were right or wrong. The issue was whether civilian control of the military should continue in this country.

I heard the General's speech from the House press gallery, looking down upon the members and looking about at many House staff members upstairs. These, the theoretically pro-President Democratic staff members and the theoretically pro-MacArthur Republican staff members, showed a common response. They wept in sympathy with the General. And even on the House floor there was an ominous tide as member after member, too, rubbed his eyes and gazed in adoration at the tall figure who had done so much for this country as a soldier but who had forgotten, understandably perhaps in the horror and frustration that was Korea, that he had a civilian superior in the President of the United States.

I assert in complete confidence and without hesitation that had an influential member suddenly offered from the floor a resolution condemning that President of the United States, and calling on General MacArthur to lead this nation forward, it could have been a bad moment for constitutional government in the United States. It could have been, that is, but for the existence of something called a Rules Committee, with a capacity for obstruction, yes, but also with a capacity for taking long thoughts and for delaying not merely wise but also unwise House decisions.

Indeed, a balanced view of the Rules Committee, formed on the basis of actual and long observation of the intractable realities as distinguished from the theoretical considerations of the case, again suggests that had it not existed *in some form* it would have had to be invented. For, as I have heretofore tried in one way or another to indicate, the genius of the House lies in the circumstance that while it rightly gives shelter to the representative system of government in its widest

and most variable forms, its very size and necessarily inchoate collective character make indispensable the existence
of a series of truly operable centers of power and responsibility within the loose outline of the whole.

To cry up "democracy" is one thing; but the greatest single
danger to the success of the democratic ideal has always been
that it might, especially in times of crisis, not be able really
to function responsibly. All this is not to say, of course, that
the Rules Committee in its current state of evolution is without fault. It has, in fact, very grave faults indeed. The principal one is that for a dozen years, at least, it has most of the
time been under the control of men sometimes prepared to
carry obstructionism to unjustified and impermissible limits
— a kind of impermissible demagoguery of its own.

In my own time as an observer of the House — an essentially friendly observer, on the whole, but one who was
and frankly remains more devoted on the whole to the Senate
as the better legislative body by and large — three Presidents have been unduly chivvied and harassed by the old
boys of Rules. "Old boys" is used not so much to suggest age
as to connote what the term "old boys" still means in some
preparatory schools — those fellows of privilege who, for
reasons both good and bad, are given great powers and
privileges within the institution.

Rules is strictly an old boys' bastion. Men are rarely, if
ever, placed upon that body unless they have demonstrated
qualities which are inherently admirable but which may
very easily be carried by extension into what is unadmirable,
indeed. They must be men of substance in the House, men of
personal strength, of high combat ability and, most of all, of

great staying power. It matters not at all whether they be eloquent, or even, in the ordinary way, of a persuasive turn of mind and character. Theirs is not always to reason why; theirs is, nearly always, to do or die.

They are not always Conservative; upon nearly any given Rules Committee will be found some of a Liberal political view. At bottom, however, it is always a Conservative group, for a number of reasons, all of which are interconnected.

In the first place there is the root fact that rural and small-town Americans still largely dominate the House, notwithstanding recent and growing court assaults upon state legislative and Congressional districting practices which have hitherto tended generally to penalize urban political interests in favor of the Jeffersonian ideal of a public society dominated by the land. In the second place, any hierarchial system tends to elevate the Conservative over the Liberal, if only because the Conservative is spiritually and intellectually more at home with the hierarchial concept and with hierarchial values. In the third place, it is simply in the nature of the Conservative animal that he makes alliances readily and naturally — with other Conservatives — to their mutual benefit. In the fourth place, the Conservative understands power — both its reality and its possibilities — with a readier instinct than that of the Liberal. The fact that he also may less understand its proper limitations is one of the reasons for the excesses of the House Rules Committee.

All this gives some insight, perhaps, into the fact that whatever else Rules may be or not be, it is incomparably the most interesting and intriguing of all House committees, always worthy of the full, fascinated attention of the man who likes to watch politics as others may like to watch plays or birds. My own awareness of this unique place opened with the end of the Second World War when, returning from observing highly unsubtle battles involving divisions and Armies, I set out, as a political correspondent, to observe the extraordinarily subtle battles, this time involving parties and fractions of parties and cliques and countercliques, which are the common business of the House Committee on Rules.

In those distant days, the chairman of the committee, who had arrived at his position by the operation of seniority, was one of those untypical committee chairmen, of whom I have previously spoken, who are allowed to reign, but not rule. This was an old boss-machine Democrat from Chicago, Adolph Sabath, who found himself a small urban and liberal island utterly surrounded by rural or small-town members, from both the Democratic and Republican parties. "Judge" Sabath (the appellation "Judge" is not infrequently bestowed by the House upon chairmen of the Rules Committee with no known past judicial distinction, perhaps because of its magisterial connotations) walked a formidable road to hard rewards. He was, upon many significant occasions, a chairman without a committee, as doggedly he sought to give faithful support to each and every legislative recommendation of President Harry S Truman, at a time when the mood of the House was anything but hospitable toward that excellent President and that incomparably poor practical politician.

When Rules would break up one of its closed meetings to announce that such and such of Mr. Truman's then famous twenty-one-point legislative program had been "acted upon," we all knew that this "action" had been negative in the extreme. Either clearance to the House floor had been refused outright, or a "rule," or clearance, had been provided in such form as to offer the pro-Truman forces very little prospect of success upon the floor of the House.

The committee had, as it still has, several options. It could bring out a bill under a "closed" rule, meaning that when the bill reached the floor all amendments were barred and it was necessary to take the whole bill or no bill at all. It could bring out a bill under an "open" rule, meaning that the general House membership could adopt amendments if it liked — and found the votes to do so. And it could lay down limitations upon the total time of debate which was to be allowed to the House — two hours, three hours, four hours, or whatnot.

In the days of the reign but not rule of "Judge" Sabath, one could confidently forecast what the scene would be when the Judge opened the committee doors to announce that such and such a measure had been "acted upon." Sitting at the head of the committee table, in a scarred, scruffy little room just off the House chamber, old Sabath would gallantly proclaim that "the most vicious rule" in all his experience had just been promulgated upon the unfortunate measure at hand. This meant either that the thing had been bottled up outright; or that — if the measure obviously was one of those which the House could not be expected simply to pass in toto with no opportunity for alteration — it had been sent out under an "open" rule.

While the Judge was passing this stern judgment upon the late action of his committee, his colleagues of Rules would sprawl in a kind of affectionate contempt around the table, hectoring him mildly as the Judge rapped for order with a gavel long since all but splintered by many such uses and cried out again and again ". . . . most vicious rule . . . most vicious rule!" A certain extra raffishness was added to the scene by the fact that the Judge, who was of Bohemian extraction, pronounced his "v's" as "w's" and thus the word "vicious" in his mouth always came out as "wicious." His colleagues would permit themselves a smile at this; but they would permit none in the onlookers. Though they did not really respect the old fellow, they liked him, even though they fought him endlessly, and they would allow no disrespect to him from "outsiders" — not excluding the "outsiders" who made up the collective membership of the House of Representatives.

There, in those days, would be Clarence Brown of Ohio, a stout, able, Old Guard Ohio Republican, a matchlessly faithful follower of the late Senator Robert A. Taft, a massively honest and massively unchangeable ultra-Conservative, totally tolerant of all Liberals as men and totally intolerant of any and all of their designs. There would be the thin, gangling William Colmer of Mississippi, an unreconstructed Southern Democrat fighting an endless rearguard action against every ideological turn in the Democratic Party as he had been brought up to know that party, say, fifty years before. There was the rugged, nasal, bald and also able Leo Allen of Illinois, the very picture, one might have thought, of a small-town midwestern American Legionnaire — who was all that, and a good deal more.

Not all of old Judge Sabath's committeemen are around

now, as I write, and the Judge himself has long since gone to whatever ultimate rewards may be bestowed upon those who are only faithful. But the little Rules Committee room still stands just as it did nearly twenty years ago; shabby, crowded, surely out of date altogether as a structure, whether or not it is somewhat out of date as the symbol of a Congressional practice. But another "Judge," this time the courtly, cultivated, memorably honorable and also memorably backward-looking Howard W. Smith of Virginia, is at the head of Rules. And though "Judge" Smith is a thousand miles away from "Judge" Sabath, in competence, in prestige, in effectiveness, there is still much in Rules which is unchanged — and perhaps forever unchangeable. Smith himself both reigns and rules; and his aristocratic presence has muted — but not yet altogether ended — that quality of raffishness, a sort of restrained rakishness, which still hovers over Rules even in the new time and the new dispensation.

16

THE OTHER GREAT COMMITTEES

THE RULES COMMITTEE still fights its interminable battles in a kind of cellar of cheerful intrigue and assassination and counterassassination where the shadows of many forces and interests — the Administration, the two political parties, the hopes and wishes of this or that Presidential aspirant who would like to see his party in the House associated with support for or opposition to this or that particular bill — crowd in with unseen presence. Unseen but present, too, are the shades of many other pressures and counterpressures; the lobbyists for labor, for industry, for agriculture, for consumer groups, for a dozen interests fighting for special places within the national interest.

The Rules Committee as it stands, as I write this, shows that unbreakable link with the past, that continuity, which makes it, as with all other institutional parts of the House, an essentially timeless instrumentality, ever changing in detail but substantially changeless in principle. Three of those members from the old days of Judge Sabath — Smith, Colmer and Brown — still sit upon it. Along with them sit others whose personalities and personal circumstances well illustrate the careful balancing of sectional and other interests which normally goes into its makeup. Its current personnel reflects, too, what is another reality in the House itself. This is that always the Republicans are less troubled by intra-party divisions, sectional or otherwise, than the Democrats.

For the Republican side of the current Rules Committee is just about what it always is — strictly orthodox Republican.

But the Democratic side of the panel shows nearly all the colors of the political spectrum in reflecting the fact that many minds and many moods make up the Democratic Party. Its two most senior members, Chairman Smith and William Colmer, symbolize the Old South and its frequent — but by no means invariable — Conservative coalitions with the Republicans. But down below this top Democratic stratum the roster proves that in the Democratic House there are, indeed, many mansions. Ray J. Madden, from an industrial area of Indiana, is a perfect representative of the urban-labor wing of the Democratic Party. James J. Delaney of New York speaks for what survives of the old-fashioned sometimes liberal-oriented and sometimes conservative-oriented Big City, Big Machine, Democratic Party so long, but no more, typified by Tammany Hall in New York City. James W. Trimble of Arkansas, Homer Thornberry of Texas and Carl Elliott of Alabama have represented the moderate wing of the Southern Democratic Party which, in an agony of effort and in enormous courage, too, is attempting to make some decent accommodation between the demands on the one side for Negro civil rights in the South and the nostalgic requirements on the other side of the old way of life in the South.

Richard Bolling of Missouri carries the brief, in part, of the Democratic liberal-intellectuals in his party. But he departs from his fellow intellectuals in some things, because a strain of practicality lies in him — who would not otherwise have ever been put upon Rules in the first place. Thomas P. O'Neill, Jr., of Massachusetts is a strictly New Frontier, or Kennedy, Democrat. B. F. Sisk of California speaks for two things — the controlling moderate Democratic liberalism of the far West and the emerging power of California as the emerging first state in electoral votes.

No one can now say what reforms will overtake Rules in the years ahead. It is surely not exempt from partial reform, as was proved by Speaker Rayburn and the Kennedy Administration in 1961, when they marshaled sufficient forces to pack the committee with enough additional members to give Rayburn ultimate control over most of its activities. But a confident forecast can be made that it will never be wholly abandoned by a House which always fears it, which sometimes hates it, but which would be lost without its power for good as well as for ill.

Whereas Rules operates within the inner framework of the House, the strictly legislative committees sit upon a wider stage, from the public point of view. Ways and Means moves most of the time with the ponderous smoothness of a large, well-organized bank. Appropriations, necessarily cut up into a long series of subcommittees having specialized training in the various main forms of appropriations to government departments and agencies, reminds one of the profound truth in American society that he who sits closest to the cash register is a good friend to have and an exceedingly bad enemy to make.

Appropriations is eternally ready to defend its powers and prestige and perquisites. This was seen embarrassingly in 1962 when the aged chairmen of House Appropriations, Clarence Cannon of Missouri, and of Senate Appropriations, Carl Hayden of Arizona, brought the whole appropriating process to a prolonged halt when they conducted a cold war of "face" as to which body should defer to the other in the matter of selecting a common meeting place for certain negotiations between the two.

My own preference among all House committees, however, on the criterion of very high expertise, is the Committee on Armed Services. The man who so long presided over it, Carl Vinson of Georgia, was uniquely *the* Mister Chairman of all the long list I myself have known. Vinson's knowledge of military affairs, after half a century in Congress and after decades as a specialist in military legislation, was a vast library of facts. The first act of the then new Secretary of Defense, Robert McNamara, after his inauguration in 1961 was to go up to the Capitol for a grave call of courtesy upon "Uncle Carl". The old gentleman, perhaps the most elite of all the elite among House Nationals, was up there in Congress long before there *was* a Pentagon. And no twist or turn in the chaotic tale of American military preparation through three wars — the First World War, the Second World War, the Korean War — escaped his monumentally faithful and incredibly perceptive eye.

He could easily have presided as that most curious of all Congressional figures, an absolute despot, if he had so chosen, but instead he was a patriarch so long suffused with the concepts of civility and fairness that the House valued him as a sort of irreplaceable treasure. He was a benign tribal leader who had a hundred times shown that most indispensable of all qualities to his followers, the capacity to lead wisely, successfully and with a high disinterestedness, for the country's safety, above all party and personal considerations. In his own person he was the one best answer to critics of the seniority system in the House.

He looked down from the chairman's seat at many Secretaries of Defense as they have come and gone. Many times he fought with them, when he thought them to be wrong. But never, win or lose, did he pursue any one of them with vindictiveness — even thought at times he found it hard not to address one or another of them as "Sonny." A kind of Roman elder to whom his country owes a hardly imaginable, and surely unimagined, debt, he bore himself with that air of self-deprecation, of a genial foxy canniness, which the House now loves, and always has. His large committee, made up of nearly two-score men, he handled with an absent-minded air masking the one thing which, finally and most of all, he personified: A deep, unsleeping sense of national and world responsibility.

Years ago, before reorganization merged the old Naval and Military (Army) Affairs committees into this present Committee on the Armed Services, old Vinson was chairman of Naval Affairs. Then he oversaw the Navy; later he oversaw it all. He was strongly suspected, upon his accession to the newly unified committee, of a pro-Navy bias. "They are saying down there at the Air Force," he told me one day in a dour voice but with a twinkling eye, "that the old man up there in Congress — me — has got on his Navy cap. Well, they better wait and see. This old man has got on three caps now (meaning Army, Navy and Air Force) and he can't any more tell one from another."

All the same, some chemical trace of his old Navy days remained. It was his habit, when a man came freshly on to his committee, to call him "Ensign." When the man had done well some legislative chore, Vinson gave him a single accolade; he called him and said "*Captain,* I am glad to talk to you again."

The Committee on the Judiciary, the biggest in the House in terms of the total number of bills that go before it, offers yet another example of the great sense of effective responsibility, as well as power, that lies in the committee system. Its chairman is, and long has been, Emanuel Celler, a man whose constituency is a thousand miles from that of Vinson in the geographic sense and thousands of miles distant in other senses. For while "Uncle Carl" spoke for an unchangingly rural district full of tenth-generation Americans of Anglo-Scottish background, "Manny" Celler speaks for a Brooklyn constituency which is a melting pot indeed. Himself cheerfully Jewish, he represents a very microcosm of that rich pluralistic mixture which has, in the last half century, become the larger face of American life — Italian, Irish, Jewish, and all the rest.

Superficially, of course, these two chairmen talked different languages, but at the true heart of the matter, the forwarding of the interest of the United States by responsible political and legislative conduct, they were of one voice and one tone. By harsh and fundamental political necessity they differed, really, on one thing alone in high public policy. By conviction and necessity, Celler presses for those Federal sanctions in the field of civil rights which by conviction and necessity Vinson opposed. But take them away from this one part of a world which neither made — the long and tragic division symbolized by the Mason-Dixon Line — and together they stood always for an informed, a fair and a reasonable promotion of the higher national concerns of this country.

Celler could easily be a mere demagogue on race, as Vinson could easily have been a mere unthinking militarist in mufti. Instead, the New Yorker tries to see to it that every issue coming before Judiciary — not excluding that of civil rights itself — is treated with that decent concern for all the nation which characterizes the House itself in its better moments. Celler understands in his field, as Vinson did in his, that the factor of consent must underlie any and all useful legislative reforms in this country. Thus while lesser men from minority-group constituencies happily turn to that most facile of all courses, an automatic acceptance of the most extreme demands of whatever may be currently the most politically powerful of minority-group pressures, Celler habitually stands fast for the responsibly attainable instead of what is irresponsibly unattainable and yet would be politically most rewarding to him personally as a Northern Congressman.

Wherever in the last decade there has been true legislative progress in civil rights this nationally obscure, but deeply valued House man has made, of all his colleagues, the largest single contribution. His contribution to achievement as distinguished from talking, by way of illustration, has been at least ten times that of the infinitely more celebrated Senator from his own state, Jacob K. Javits, though "Manny" Celler could walk nearly any street in New York City, probably including some streets in his own bailiwick of Brooklyn, and pass entirely unnoticed.

But, for purposes of contrast, turn now to the one "major" House committee which can be so described only by the courtesy of long custom, the Committee on Foreign Affairs. This extraordinary body is, in fact, a long-standing and thus persistently uncorrected error, an enduring solecism in what is otherwise a strong and logical committee system. The more I have watched it and reflected upon it, the less reason I can see for its existence.

In theory, it shares Congressional jurisdiction over foreign policy matters with the powerful and imperious Senate Committee on Foreign Relations. (There is a time-worn jest at the Capitol that the difference in nomenclature is this: while the House Committee is at least theoretically capable of having affairs, the Senate committee is manifestly incapable of having relations, if not because of its age, then because of its profound love of itself.)

In theory the House Committee on Foreign Affairs vies with the Senate Committee on Foreign Relations in helping the President prepare and implement our varying foreign policies. All Administrations perforce adhere to this solemn fiction. Secretaries of State go gravely up to the Hill to report to Foreign Affairs, as to Foreign Relations, and to seek the advice and counsel of Foreign Affairs, as of Foreign Relations.

The distinction in truth is that when Administration witnesses go to the Senate committee they really do go to report the past and to seek guidance for the future. But when they go before House Foreign Affairs they go really because it is part of an ancient game of deference to a committee whose title far exceeds its power or purpose. Accordingly, most of the sessions held by Foreign Affairs are touched with an inescapable air of tentativeness and of basic unreality. The policy makers from "Downtown" must touch base there, because that has always been the thing to do. But the real business between Administration and Capitol Hill only begins when Foreign Relations is the locus and arena.

This is not, of course, to say that there are not able men presently on Foreign Affairs, or that there have not been many able men on it in the past. But it is to say that the whole makeup of the House, the whole nature of the House, makes this one committee a kind of vermiform appendix. The House is basically incapable, save on rare occasions, of conducting a truly sensible and grand debate on foreign policy. Its inherent interests lie elsewhere; and its rules and procedures do not encourage great dialogues upon foreign affairs, over which in the end it has the very considerable power of the public purse, but that power alone.

The great distinction is that the Constitution gives to the Senate an intimate form of power over foreign affairs that it has never given to the House. The Senate can accept or reject treaties entered into by a President; it thus has a great hand, always, in the very making of those treaties through the Constitutional provision which requires it to "advise" the President and allows it to withhold its "consent." The same goes, of course, for all major diplomatic appointments made by the President, from the Secretary of State downward.

The House therefore stands outside the game both in its "advice" and "consent" aspects; it comes into the arena only when it is time to put up the money for what has already in fact been decided upon by President and Senate. All the same, the House Foreign Affairs Committee goes on. It has, at minimum, some point of early contact with the decision-making process in foreign policy, if only because of those faithful, and often actually pointless, calls which the men from "Downtown" must make upon it. And it provides committee berths for members who might otherwise be hard to accommodate in the committee system. Some prestige, some cachet, always attaches to Foreign Affairs: Its members are made to feel part of the great movements of the world, are invited to Embassies and, somewhat casually, deferred to socially in those countless Washington functions in which the State Department has some part. To be placed upon Foreign Affairs is, after all, not so bad as to be fobbed off with membership on, let us say, the House committee on the affairs of the District of Columbia.

IV

THE STRENGTHS
AND THE
WEAKNESSES

17

THE HOUSE AND THE WHITE HOUSE

EVER SINCE the last two years of Herbert Hoover's brief Presidential tenure — when, led by Speaker John N. Garner, it became the spearhead of an implacable partisan attack upon Mr. Hoover — the House of Representatives has been wholly overshadowed in the public mind. The fact that it has taken second place to the Presidency has been both understandable and inevitable. For the powers of the Presidency, from Franklin D. Roosevelt's time forward — and not even excluding the period of the rather relaxed use of that office by Dwight D. Eisenhower — have been so steadily increased and so steadily asserted from the White House that they have long since become the clearly dominant powers within the old triune and theoretically coequal structure of the American government, Executive, Legislative, Judicial. It could not have been otherwise. The onset in the thirties of the twin scourges of Nazi-Fascist terrorism and worldwide economic depression created political conditions which overshadowed all mere political theories for the most compellingly simple of all reasons: iron necessity. The paralysis of Depression required an executive leadership, which is to say an essentially one-man leadership, that could see the problem as nothing less than a *national* disaster and so act upon it with a single-mindedness approaching economic and political martial law. The diffused general character of the House made it during the worst of the crisis an imperfect instrument for dealing with a national economic illness so virulent as to require remedies outside the experience of this corporate body. The Great Depression was an economic collapse so much more severe than we had ever known before that the difference in degree became in fact a difference in principle.

Moreover, the very act of breaking the paralysis set in motion irreversible changes and forces which would forever make it impossible for the American Presidency to draw back from or to relinquish the emergency powers it had arrogated to itself in the course of the struggle. Those old "emergency powers" now have long since become the accustomed and rarely debated powers of the Presidency in ordinary times.

At the height of the hurricane, the House perforce surrendered forever much of its old inheritance of critical decision-making.

In approving the Hull Reciprocal Tariff program it accepted the beginning of the end of its historic grip over tariff-making. In passing varied labor and social welfare legislation of the Roosevelt time (pensions, unemployment compensation as a permanent feature of economic life, and so on), it opened the way to a new concept of the management-labor contest as an explicitly national concern. In this context there became all but irrelevant that important aspect of the life of the House which is inherent in the localized and sharply separated Congressional districts.

And in agreeing to the creation of scores of executive bureaus and commissions exercising powers theretofore held largely or solely by Congress itself, the House sped the process. In short, circumstances made the country an increasingly Federalized, an increasingly homogenized society; a society moving away from the scheme of fragmented, district-by-district, power which is one of the bases upon which the House stands.

What was true of the economic crisis was even more true of the world crisis of which Hitler was both evil creator and frightening symbol. The House, because of its essential lack of power in foreign policy except at the point of signing the checks, and because it is at the last only a *home* place, necessarily sank in the scale of public estimation with every increase in Hitlerism's menace to the world. *This* was not the place to deal with Hitler. The Presidency was the place. And this truth was grasped by the instinct of the people as well as being overtly driven into their consciousness by the steadily rising dramatic value of the Presidency's role.

And again, as in the case of the Great Depression which changed so much before it had run its course, pre-emptive Presidential powers assumed for the duration of the Second World War remained unaltered when it had ended — because they must.

If all these observations make it fairly clear why the House has so fallen under the shadow of the Presidency in the last three decades, the explanation of its subordination in public regard to the Senate is not so easy. Within this writer's own lifetime, "Congress" to most people really meant simply the House; the Senate was generally seen as a remote and even somewhat mysterious instrumentality brought to wide public notice only periodically and episodically. Senator Borah of Idaho could keep the stage with his isolationist foreign views. Senator Walsh of Montana could enliven the public with his investigations of scandal in the Harding Administration, Senator Nye of North Dakota with his earnest howling against "the merchants of death" (the munitions makers). And so on. But on the whole, in those far-off days, the people looked to the House as their *Congress,* as the place where their real affairs were largely settled. Most of the time, the Senate was something no doubt very important; but also slightly theatrical and not, really, of the domestic scene.

In looking back upon it, it seems to me that this position began to change during the time of Franklin Roosevelt — that author, consciously or not, of so many changes. More specifically, the elevation of the Senate to the relative derogation of the House started, I believe, when, in his second term, Roosevelt, from the best possible motives, made the greatest and most enduring domestic mistake in a generally brilliant career. This was his attempt to pack the Supreme Court. It early became evident to the reasonably perceptive that whether this attempt was to be defeated or approved, the Senate and not the House would be the decisive arena. For the issue posed was not mercantile or bread-and-butter (a true House interest in dealing with which House expertise is incomparably high), but Constitutional. Officially, Congress, as one part of the triune system, was one of the antagonists; the Court the second, and the Presidency the third.

In fact, however, the President's one real antagonist instantly became neither the Court nor the House but the Senate. This was the way it had to be. What was first of all required was a great and sustained national debate, for nothing less than a Constitutional crisis and a crisis in national tradition was at hand.

For such a debate, over so vast and yet so intangible a field of affairs, the House, as I have tried to show, is inherently ill-equipped. It is far from incapable of exploring, ventilating and elaborating many issues. But it is rarely capable of a deep, creative examination and counterexamination of the kind that was then demanded — an inquest upon imponderables involved in a question of measureless moment around which there were no unchallengeably fixed points of reference.

The rules of the House, its size and largely superficial but nevertheless distracting confusions, its whole corporate personality, demand that its debates proceed from at least some measurable data. It requires if not mundane premises, at least premises subject to purely objective analysis. Would a tax cut, say, in fact raise productivity and if so, where and to what degree? Wherein would this bill dealing with agricultural subsidies profit the farm economy? How much, if anything, would it mean in the way of undesirably extended Federal controls? Who profits here, and who loses? All such questions (and by no standard are they mean or niggling questions) the House can handle with skill and dispatch.

18

FOREIGN POLICY

BUT WHAT if the issue is not as to which section or interest — or district — profits or loses, even in the higher sense of these terms? What if it involves, rather, the immense and the formless, such as the right values to be placed upon Constitutional tradition on the one hand and upon the urgent needs of a national executive on the other? What then? At such a point, the House cannot, as the sonorously decorous phrase goes in the United Nations, really seize itself of the issue. What "rule" for two or four or even six hours of debate, whether "open" or "closed," will open such a box and display all that lies within it, having in mind that some of what is in it is visible only to the mind's eye and by the power of sustained imagery and allusion?

Members may rise and cry "Mister Speaker" and obtain his recognition and speak their piece. It may be a quite good piece; and often it is. But there is, and can be, nothing in this forum which gives spiritual space for that leisured deliberation, that endless crossfire of assertion and retort, that unhurried reflection which in the truly grand debates of our national life make the Senate process a memorable thing, no matter how one may feel about the conclusions which that body at last draws.

The accounting thus far shows three reasons why the House has lost something of its old public place — though it retains a great and enduring place: depression on a heretofore unknown scale; World War of a heretofore unimagined scope and ferocity; the House's own inherent incapacity to deal effectively with the highly generalized and subtle Constitutional issues arising in a century which is both increasingly brutal and increasingly sophisticated in the complexity of the questions it poses.

The true mission (and the true story) of all high national politics in America since the end of the Second World War has been the proper conduct of the cold war, as the one true goal of national politics has been the salvation of this country in the immense and seemingly endless struggle between that part of the world which is substantially self-governing, and thus denominated as the Free World, and that part which is in the dour embrace of the massive and malignant non-government of international, imperialist Communism.

It would be far too much to say that as this struggle has unfolded, the House of Representatives has become irrelevant. It plays, indeed, an indispensable part. For the House is still the legislative forum in which, most of all, are made those climactic decisions in our domestic affairs by which the nation's posture toward the world is allowed to stand upon a firm or less than firm home base.

But the role is secondary to the cutting edge of national

policy abroad, as the role of supply in a military operation is secondary to the cutting edge of the combat echelons. The critical forward line in this historic battle of foreign policy is held, necessarily, by the Presidency. The Senate forms a second operational line. It may be seen as a mobile reserve which, while not immediately in contact with the enemy, is nevertheless a combat mass of maneuver as distinguished from a merely logistical force of support. In this matter of matchless gravity, in short, the House of Representatives is necessarily the quartermaster's corps. Essential to the action? Indeed it is. A part of the action? Indeed so; but, all the same, a part of the action which, while vital to its success, helps execute, but cannot establish, either the strategy or the tactics of the operation.

So, to drop a military metaphor which in any event is applicable only in a loosely illustrative way, the changes brought by this century in the world's essential conditions have necessarily lowered the power and consequence of the House over that set of affairs — world policy — which has taken a more or less permanent first place in the mind and concerns of the Republic.

As a close, and on the whole a fond, observer of this old House I have never heard there a truly memorable, truly illuminating debate upon the great foreign policy questions which have both enlivened and bedeviled the era in which we live. But I have heard a hundred sharp, acute, hard and knowing discussions on public works programs, public and private power, agricultural subsidies, housing and welfare programs — a hundred trenchant and able dialogues upon such home concerns of this nation.

To ask of the House the kind of foreign policy debate, or grand Constitutional inquest, which can be heard in the Senate at its best, is like asking an able and elderly banker or farmer, a man deeply and perfectly at home with the realities of banking or farming, to turn his efforts to an imaginative, creative discussion of, say, the doctrine of transsubstantiation. When the House is thrust into the great, swampy fields of world affairs the result is rarely a happy one.

To give a small contemporary illustration, ponder the contributions of the House (the Republican side of the House in this instance) to the principal Republican Congressional counterpropaganda to the Kennedy and Johnson Administrations. This has been called, irreverently, "the Ev and Charlie Show," after the names of its two participants, the Republican Senate leader, Senator Everett McKinley Dirksen of Illinois, and the House Republican leader, Representative Charles Halleck of Indiana.

Messrs. Dirksen and Halleck made a habit of meeting periodically with the national press to give the Republican version of current political affairs. The "Charlie" of this enterprise, Representative Halleck, is beyond doubt one of the ablest, toughest party floor leaders of modern times. When he and "Ev" centered their joint efforts upon domestic criticism of the Administration their performance was an impressive one, whether or not one agreed with its premises. But when the theme of their appearance was foreign policy the "Ev" part becomes, immediately and perceptibly, the far more valid role in the show. The "Charlie" here — and this is due to no fault of his own — was less than impressive on these occasions. For "Charlie" was working and speaking here outside the area of his true competence; he was playing the wrong game in the wrong field.

Only the rare House member (for examples, Walter Judd, mentioned earlier; William Fulbright of Arkansas, later a United States Senator) can take significantly creative roles in foreign affairs in the House.

For all these reasons discussions in philosophic terms of foreign affairs in the House take on both a certain unrealism and a touch of stereotyped thinking and action. Any enduring and recurring issue in this field — say the complicated question of whether and how much to extend American economic aid to Soviet satellites, produces neither great light nor genuine heat.

In such a scene, the House, quite frankly, is the home of a hundred clichés, a hundred oversimplifications of the matter at hand. The outcome is, most often, a charade, albeit a desperately earnest one in which members are acting out character parts — Hard Liners, Soft Liners, and so on — rather like children in a school Christmas play solemnly but unconvincingly representing themselves to be bad Ebenezer Scrooges, or good Bob Cratchits, or even, in some cases, Tiny Tims.

The implications of all of this are not lost on members, most of whom are entirely sensible men. Being early instructed in the root truth that the House can more readily unmake (by withholding the requisite money) than make foreign policy, the ablest men — for the most part — early turn their efforts away from this ill-rewarding field toward the true and vital concerns of their place. The exceptions, the men whose singular interest in foreign affairs must persist in spite of themselves, will in nearly every case either remove themselves in time to the Senate or strive mightily to do so. William Fulbright was one of these; he left the House to become a Senator who in due course, by the operation of seniority, reached his present eminence as chairman of the Senate Committee on Foreign Relations.

The current majority leader of the Senate, the able Montana Democrat, Senator Mike Mansfield, took a similar course, taking care after he reached the position of party headship to remain a member of the Foreign Relations Committee. In that Other Body, Mansfield and Fulbright are men of both power and distinction. Had they remained in the House it is most likely that both would today be pretty dim figures, well down among House Average in terms of both influence and personal position.

19

THE SENATE MAN IN THE HOUSE

THUS, the central strength of the House, its great capacity
to deal in pragmatic effectiveness with those home concerns
which are its real business, carries the seed of one of its
greatest weaknesses. This is its inherent incapacity to bring
forward its men of talent where those talents lie outside that
less than comprehensive but far from small area in which
House competence can truly exert itself.

One of the great parliamentary figures of our time, President Lyndon Johnson, was competent but never outstanding in his days in the House for a related reason. Though
he was not in those early days overly concerned with the
world's dominant business, the cold war, his extraordinary
ability was never fully developed in the House. This latent
ability, later so brilliantly shown in the Senate, was to produce or force a consensus among his colleagues, by working
as an *individual*, a political entrepreneur, in a way which is
impossible within the rather stilted forms of collective leadership on which depend both order and performance in the
House.

Where the House is constitutionally (and also to some extent Constitutionally, with a capital "c") unable to deal subtly with the subleties of world affairs, it is also inherently unable to adapt itself to the more fluid forms of political leadership which the very able, at any rate, can develop within the Senate. Seniority and respect for constituted authority are powerful forces in both chambers; but in the Senate the really superior man can find means to detour the one, all the while bowing to it with all grace and deference, and to infiltrate the other so that the constituted authority becomes his ally rather than a repressive force to him. Johnson became a member of the Senate hierarchy before he had been a year in that body, simply by virtue of a high capacity for personal leadership which would have done him little good in the House for yet another dozen years.

The House is not so much lacking in regard for the odd political genius as it is simply too crowded, both by numbers and by its great mass of quite necessary rules and regulations, to give the brilliant individualist leader room to prove himself and to develop his expertise. The House marches; the Senate thinks, and sometimes overlong. And then it slowly and absentmindedly saunters down the corridors of history, taking time to examine not merely the scenes presently upon view and to put the mind's eye ahead to the future turnings, but also to reflect quietly upon the turnings that the past has brought.

The House is the home neither of justice nor injustice; it is the home of action, usually sound, and reaction, often automatic. The Senate occasionally is the home of great injustice, as when so long it permitted the late Senator Joseph McCarthy to run amuck among men's reputations and liberties. But sometimes it is also the last and bravest home of justice, especially when justice is everywhere else denied by those passions which may seize majorities as well as minorities. It is hard to bring the House to approve a bill of impeachment; but, given a certain public atmosphere of anger and clamor, it is not impossible. Under such a public lash, the House impeached President Andrew Johnson of Tennessee (one of the historical favorites, he once told me, by the way, of another President called Harry S Truman) for the high crime of trying to carry out the wise and compassionate post-Civil War policies of Abraham Lincoln. But a Senate of the United States, under the same public lash, could not be whipped or dragooned emotionally enough or long enough to vote the Bill of Impeachment; and the country was thus saved a stain upon its record which not all the following centuries could have rubbed out.

The House, again, is both more democratic and less democratic than the Other Body — to which I make much comparative reference both for purposes of illustrations and because it is not possible to describe one half of an egg without saying something here and there about the other half.

It is more democratic in several senses. The will of a majority, even a bare majority, may be worked in the House without undue delay. Though the power of obstruction by the Rules Committee is a real power, it is also a power upon which real and readily definable limits have been set. The grip of Rules upon any measure can be shattered at any time that a mere majority-by-one of the House is ready to sign a petition to discharge that committee from further control over the measure. Thus, there is only a partial analogy between Rules in the House and the filibuster in the Senate. For no Senate rule guarantees an end to filibustering short of the marshaling of a two-thirds vote to apply the cloture, or gag.

House members, moreover, are usually in fact (but sometimes only in theory) "closer to the people." Their limited tenure of two years, as against six years for a Senator, is presumed to keep their ears closer to the ground — to the sacred "grass roots" of our political mythology. Their procedures are ostensibly directed, singly and simply, toward a single, simple result: the gathering of a mere numerical majority in behalf of a proposition.

Too, the almost bucolic simplicity of House life and work style, compared to the more sophisticated living and working style of the Senate, is widely assumed to have, in itself, a special democratic virtue. In this, as in some other qualities of the House, there is a nostalgic recall of this country's distant yesteryears as an essentially frontier community everywhere beyond the Appalachians to the West and everywhere westward of tidewater in the South.

Over the proceedings of the House and of its committees, and over the personal life of members, there is a home folks, or workshop, aura that is not present in the Senate or among Senators. This is necessarily the case. As we have seen, the House usually takes a back seat to the Senate in the great foreign policy enterprises which are the most urgent public concerns of our years. The Senate also usually conducts those spotlight investigations which come and go on Capitol Hill.

There is also the fact that individual House members are rarely so noticed by the press — including the society columns — as are individual Senators. And there is, most of all, the fact that at the very end of any legislative enterprise even the greatest House member casts the vote of one man out of 435 whereas the meanest member of the Senate casts one vote out of 100 — and also half the vote of an entire state.

Since the House is no place for prima donnas it is, and can be, no place for that rich element of theater — sometimes good and sometimes bad theater — which invests all but the dullest of Senate proceedings. Lacking the true capacity to produce great drama and limited by its rules and traditions and operating processes mainly to plodding work in the mass, the House perforce also lacks that quality of style — and particularly of individual style — which can be seen across the Capitol. Urgent it can sometimes be; ornate it cannot be.

We have had a long persisting theory that prairie democracy (along, of course, with that other emotional concept, "the New England Town Meeting") was somehow necessarily purer and more authentically democratic than all others. These articles of faith were always of doubtful validity; as of now they do more credit to our sentiment than to our sense of reality.

Thus the truth of the business is that the quotient of democracy is higher in the House only if one assumes "democracy" to mean the nearest possible approach to a kind of Gallup poll majority rule which is fearful and even somewhat resentful of minority views — and only if one assumes that the House actually proceeds in this way. But of course it does not.

For the simplicity of the working style of the House is by no means simplistic; and the marshaling and the counting of the bodies pro and con are by no means the mere Gallup poll process they might appear. The genius of James Madison of Virginia, the true father of the Constitution so long overshadowed in memory by the far more pretentious and far more precious Thomas Jefferson, still gleams, if largely by accident, through the actual working processes of the House. Madison's great gift to rational and responsible government, of course, was the careful raising up of a series of interlocking but separate governmental arms and power structures deliberately designed for perpetual intercompetition and thus for more or less perpetual check-and-balance.

Though he had not meant to carry this precise plan down onto the very floor of the House, where he himself served for a time with a somewhat glum and absentminded distinction, the years and the generations of experience have carried it there anyhow. For the ultimate and greatest strength of the House as an institution is the fact that it has, over rather more than a century and a half, adapted, and adopted to itself, that system of check-and-balance.

20

EFFECTIVE MANEUVER

CHECK-AND-BALANCE operates in the House not primarily through its rules (though it does, in fact, in the single instance of the Rules Committee) but more through its inbuilt, tactile understanding that this is the way in which the enterprise must, in fact, be run. The creation of an effective majority for any highly important and highly disputed bill is a far more complicated process than merely sending out the party Whips to beat and cajole the rank-and-file, as is usually done in the British House of Commons.

Effective majorities are created in such cases much as a great mosaic is made. Many prismatic stones will be required, of many, divergent and essential colors. The immediate objective is not the instant finding of some flat, horizontal consensus; if at this stage there are both lumps and improbably streaky and clashing tones on the face of the mural that is a matter of no great account. The immediate objective, instead, is more to smooth out the stone surface upon which the mural is to be laid than to set in the mosaic pieces themselves.

The first problem, in the House, is not to discover the precise strength of the bill on its intrinsic merits. It is, instead, coolly to calculate the degree of resistance to it, the true nature and causes of that resistance, and the probable means by which these natures and these causes can be so altered or abated as to make it possible to look forward to the ultimate acceptance and completion of a grand design.

To put the thing more concretely, say that circumstances have led the hierarchs of the controlling party in the House to conclude, however reluctantly, that fundamental labor reform has become both a vital legislative issue and a national necessity. Assume that, in this case, the hierarchs of the House are of the same party as the President in the White House (though it would be much the same if they were of a different party).

Informal and exploratory negotiations between these hierarchs and the man in the White House will then be opened. The man in the White House will at length agree in principle that labor reform is needed. Or perhaps he will disagree; in any event, the essential approach of the House hierarchs will not be greatly altered, granted the basic assumption that they have conclusively and unalterably determined upon labor reform as an unavoidable Congressional obligation. In the case of a disagreeing President they will not be halted; they will only be deflected. They will set out bargaining with him in the way in which they will later bargain with dissident or reluctant House members. Their purpose will be to begin to disengage his hostility to the point where at length he will say: Very well, I am really against the whole idea; but if you insist upon going

into this thing at all you may do such and such with my reluctant consent, but you must on no account attempt to
do so and so. Whether he says substantially this, or whether
instead he gives his full and ready consent to what is afoot,
the hierarchs will proceed from there on in about the same
way.

They will then put the matter before the House Labor Committee; whose chairman will, of course, be himself one of
the hierarchs, so that in a sense he is at this point instructing
himself to lay hold of the issue, and, through himself, so
instructing his committee. The traditional kind of work will
ensue: long and objectively thorough hearings — a painfully
complete inquest in which many witnesses on all relevant
sides will be patiently heard. House committees generally
do give a full and fair hearing to all parties in interest. This
is not so much a gesture of nobility as one of prudent self-
interest and self-protection. It does nobody any good, any
time, in the House, to bear some responsibility for a legislative issue and not at the same time to have given himself the
maximum exposure to all possible implications and evalua-
tions and evolutions of it.

All this, however, will only begin the process of the development of a great consensus. While the winds of outside
pressures blow inward upon the committee, the seemingly
softer, but also very powerful, winds of crystallizing opinions
within the committee will blow outward from it. These will
blow not so much upon the wide public, nor even so much
upon the immediately interested and contending formal
pressure groups, as upon the large and sometimes seemingly
moon-faced, but rarely moon-minded membership of the
House.

The generality of the House will begin to inform itself of the attitudes now taking shape within the committee, at this point largely by a process of eyes-open, ears-open osmosis. It will not be conclusively influenced thereby; but it will commence to take note of the provisional consensuses now tentatively forming within the committee. A faint spirit of follow-the-leader — to a point — will now begin to manifest itself among the House generality, if in a very tentative, very hesitant, way. This is so because very few House committees, if any at all, are ever really corporately foolish; and because almost no major committee chairman, however suspiciously "liberal" to the conservatives or however darkly "conservative" to the liberals, is *ever* a mere fool.

Now that matters have reached this creatively intermediate point, the House hierarchs who want the bill, no less than the House hierarchs who don't want the bill, will begin to exercise their own version of the Madisonian principle of check-and-balance. The pro-Nationals will start moving about among the generality of the House, first, of course, among its relatively more powerful and influential members. Their motive will be to placate, to abate, to reassure, to promise reward for faithful conduct in behalf of this great measure. The anti-Nationals will start the same kind of moving about among the same kinds of members, for a precisely opposite motive: To exacerbate, to harden resistance, to warn of perils, to speak in vinegar of punishment for those unworthy fellows who may be seduced by the sweet oils being poured upon them by the pros and so elect to support this monstrous bill.

If the Speaker is among the pros — and by definition he usually is, for the bill would hardly be on the real docket of the House in the first place without his open or covert consent — members will begin to be summoned casually to one of his offices for coffee and conversation, for flattery and persuasion. To Jones it will be pointed out, perhaps, that while he is still not very senior on the committee of his own service, there are glittering opportunities in the House for a bright young fellow who does his homework, is faithful to his obligations — and is wise enough to see with clear judgment what is wise and what is unwise legislation.

This enormously complicated process *is* the legislative process and by it is endlessly re-established the fact that in making the laws under this form of government, it is the President who proposes but it is Congress which must dispose. Because it produces an endlessly varying series of consent coalitions, and also because it produces varying checks and gainsayings to the Presidency, an articulate professorial and reformist view of increasing power is urging, with great superficial appeal but in profound wrongheadedness, that this process is among the weaknesses of the House. It is, in fact, one of its most significant strengths.

21

CHECKS AND BALANCES

IT IS SUGGESTED that these shifting coalitions of consensus are untidy because they run counter to what is called party responsibility — because, let us say, all the House Democrats do not always stand with a Democratic President. They *are* untidy; but they are also both indispensable and highly effective. For party responsibility is in fact less a reality than an idealized concept in a system which is not, after all, a parliamentary one and *was never intended to be one.* Complaints of a lack of "party responsibility" proceed from vestigial enchantment with an old error — the assumption that the American system of three consciously distinct arms of government is somehow comparable to a British system which places all government in a single, merged parliamentary-executive arm. The critics are complaining that a pear is not an apple; and thus that the pear is somehow inferior to the apple.

Moreover, even within the apple itself — the British Parliamentary apple — the worm of doubt nowadays is that "party responsibility" has been carried altogether too far. When the *Times* of London, sedate, class-conscious, immensely powerful among the old elite of England, and the brash, the vulgar and the proletarian *Daily Mirror* of London agree upon any point of political philosophy, it is odd indeed.

Nevertheless, recently the *Times* sounded its well-bred thunder, seconded gustily by the cheerfully vulgar *Mirror:*

> The executive has taken over power from Parliament. It rules, or fails to rule, by a tacit agreement with outside forces in the community that their authority also shall not be challenged.

At the moment of the appearance of this editorial — challenging the excessive will to power of a Prime Minister supported by the *Times* itself, Harold Macmillan — there had just occurred a harsh debate in Commons. Its focus, according to a dispatch in the Washington *Post*, which is no friend of American Congressional authority and is in fact in the forefront of the reformist forces, was this:

> . . . The *tight party discipline* that squashes the *initiative of individual MP's, their tendency to vote blind without listening to the issues* . . .

Still, it may be objected that the *Times* of London is not sufficiently "forward-looking" and thus might be suspect as a commentator on this issue. Listen, then, to the *Manchester Guardian*, which is "forward-looking" indeed:

> As things are at the moment, the whole weight of the Government (meaning of its bureaucratic agents) is thrown on the side of the Cabinet Minister and his officials against the collective wisdom of the House of Commons. Ministers oc-

casionally concede a point under pressure, but why should
not the Commons be allowed to shape legislation, to contra-
dict a department, or to express an opinion on an issue of
policy . . . ?

The energies of Parliament would be revitalized and re-
leased *once its authority to criticize and check the Government was restored to it. It is along these lines that reform
must be pressed. The Executive will resist, because an active and powerful House of Commons will create difficulties.
That is what it is constitutionally supposed to do.*

It is suggested — and most ably so by Professor James Mac-
Gregor Burns in a brilliantly wrong book called *The Deadlock of Democracy* which places him at the intellectual headship of the reformists — that Congressional independence of
a President amounts automatically to Congressional obstructionism. This assumes that a President, if he is a "strong"
President, is necessarily right in his programs and that skeptical attitudes toward such programs necessarily involve ob-
solete thinking or obsolescent attitudes. And "strong" Presidents in this concept are not hard to define. They are such
Presidents as have "liberal" views — though the term is one
of immensely differing meanings to different men and though
two generally denominated "liberal" Presidents in our own
lifetime, Franklin Roosevelt and Harry Truman, were in simple fact poles apart on some of the most vital questions of
this century.

It assumes, too, that real progress will only be made once
Congress has been brought to heel by a variety of reforms —
destruction of the seniority system, of the Rules Committee;
in truth the replacement of the whole present hierarchial
system by another hierarchial system made up of what? Of

"representative, responsible and vigorous party policy committees under the leadership of elected party officials and their whips."

"Party officials" are in fact already "elected," and party policy committees are already surely "vigorous" at least. They are also highly "responsible." And they are unrepresentative only if one assumes that a political point of view which is demonstrably in a very thin minority in the House — the ultra-liberal point of view — should dominate nevertheless.

Moreover, the truth is that any reform of the kind proposed by Burns and by a good many others would within five years of its acceptance be no reform at all. The realities of legislative life in the House — in any foreseeable House — will not accommodate themselves to theoretical designs resting upon such splendid abstractions as "progressive . . . forward-looking" — designs formed far from the scene of daily action.

For the House is no more able — even if it were willing, as it is not now and never will be — to repeal the claims of seniority than any human enterprise is able to repeal the claims of the synonyms of seniority: experience, capacity, earned prestige, personal influence through personal power. The new "party officials" would very shortly be the old "party officials." The new "elected party leaders of Congress, working with the President" would "work with the President," as did the old, whenever, and only whenever, they had cause to do so from all that amalgam of impulses which moves the old leaders — considerations of whether the President was right in addition to being President; whether he had the country with him or against him; whether what he sought was attainable; whether Congress generally in any event would accept what he sought. And so on.

For the House of Representatives is not the President; the President is not the House of Representatives. And the function of Congress is not the function of the White House, nor will it ever be unless and until the Constitution is totally altered and the House is given power to elect a Prime Minister of this country.

Moreover, this state of affairs does not deny to the public generally some alleged "right" to have a President and Congress working harmoniously, the second in subjection to the first. For it does not follow that any President speaks, on *legislative* issues, for an overwhelming majority of the people — or even, necessarily, for any majority at all. Dwight Eisenhower won election by a vast majority in 1952, and in 1954, at the height of his own acceptability, lost that Republican Congress which under the reformists' philosophy should have been "working" with him. He was not, in truth, sorry to see it go; for the ensuing two years of an opposition Democratic Congress, with all its institutional independence, served his designs far better than what he had lost would have done. Again, in 1956, he was re-elected upon one of the greatest landslides in history — and both Houses of Congress stayed Democratic. Was the situation tidy? No. Did it reflect that the voters really wanted this almost matchlessly popular President to have his own Congress "working" with him? Hardly. They would have had only to say so, and they did not.

It is the strength of the House, and not its weakness, that it performs as a *legislative* chamber, skeptical, critical, independent, and not as a mere arm of some President and of some national partisan instrumentality called a party. For a political party is not what the reformists think it is. It is not a "conscience," but rather a form of pressure. It is not a "mind," but rather an expression of hope. It is neither "good" nor "bad"; it is only a hammer in the hands of men capable of governing; a device and not a principle.

22

THE REFORMERS

AGAIN, a strength (and never a weakness) of the House lies in the very fact that it is — to the degree that it can so remain under the blows of court decisions deciding how Congressional districts shall be formed — a redoubt against a total and ultimate control of politics by the urban society. "Malapportionment" does exist in the House, measured in strictly arithmetic terms. But a greater "malapportionment" exists in both the nomination and election of any President. The electoral power of the vast urbanized States — New York, California, Pennsylvania, Illinois, and, increasingly, also of Texas — has loaded the dice for urban man. Already, he controls not merely the Presidency, but the source materials for it. Something is surely needed to keep urban man from running away entirely with the game. If there is no inherent virtue in being small and rural, there is no necessarily saintly quality in being large and urban and demanding.

No one need go so far as to argue that the pastoral society is still with us. But, speaking of disproportions, no one aware of the human facts can possibly deny that the surviving remnants of this pastoral society do in fact provide in the old House an enormously disproportionate share of its ablest and best leaders, its men of the truest national views and the widest political horizons. It is a fact, however unwelcome, that 5 percent of the American population provides at least 50 percent of the best men in the House, not merely through the operations of seniority but through some mysterious truth which seems to operate, year in and year out, against Megalopolis as a training ground for statesmanship. Explain it fully, I cannot; assert it as the simple truth I must, upon the basis of long personal observation.

Nor is this situation really unique or necessarily anachronistic. In the highly modern democratic society of Israel, for example, the rural population has in parliament a representation five times greater than that population's mere numbers would justify. Moreover, though the farm areas amount to less than 4 percent of the total population, the rural members exercise an enormously disproportionate leadership influence quite comparable to the influence of the numerically small areas in our own House of Representatives. Indeed, as I write, 40 percent of the *Cabinet* of Israel is provided by 3.8 percent of the people of Israel.

No one who really knows the House, whatever his own ideological bent and whatever his own point of view as to the proper relationship between the Executive and the Congressional powers, can deny that the House delegates from such supreme examples of Megalopolis as New York, Philadelphia, Los Angeles and Chicago are on the whole of consistently poor relative value in terms of industry, of intellect, of political capacity and sense of national responsibility. Whenever a really striking House man arises among them the circumstance is cause for wonder and a certain tolerant incredulity among the general run of House members — not excluding those from Megalopolis itself.

Every Speaker this writer has known in the last two decades has had to deal with this human reality. Indeed, there is an old House jest about the "Tuesday-till-Thursday Club." This is a club limited to members from Megalopolis, which earned its name because of the members' tendency to take long weekends in their home cities and to spare only a three-day week for their responsibilities in Washington.

Equally well known is the even more striking tendency of members from Megalopolis happily to rid themselves from even the palest of the pale cast of thought in mortgaging their votes in advance on certain types of issues to certain "nationality" or other interest blocs in total disregard not only of national interest but of the "responsible" party leadership of their own party's White House occupant. To be more specific: every President since the Second World War has found megalopolitan members of his own party voting automatically for Polish-American, Irish-American, German-American, Italo-American or other ethnic-grouping manifestos in utterly demagogic rejection of the necessities of the nation's contemporary foreign policy.

It would, for another example, be interesting, if forbiddingly exhausting, to tot up the number of times in the last forty years in which megalopolitan votes have been cast with the utmost lightheartedness in favor of such proposed acts of madness as these: quasi declarations of war upon perfidious England (in obedience to professional-Irish sentiment), or absurd strictures on the rightful powers of the Presidency to deal responsibly with such of the Soviet-overrun central powers as Poland and Yugoslavia, in deference to Polish-American and Croatian-Serbian-American emotions against the Communist conquerors which, while entirely understandable, would simply paralyze American efforts to distinguish between voluntary and involuntary Communism in the ultimate hope of widening all possible fissures within the structure of international Communism.

Now, criticisms such as these should not be unaccompanied by a plain acknowledgment that these so-called "national interest" groups have every right to forward their views. There is no slightest trace in these observations of the nonsensical notion of the alleged superiority of "Anglo-Saxon" Congressional constituencies; the rich mixture of our national political and cultural heritage is, I have always thought, perhaps our greatest glory.

It is, however, a fact that in foreign policy issues megalopolitan Congressmen generally act without due regard for what might rightly be called the merged national interest. And it also should be said that the ruralists in the House themselves often act, on yet other issues, against that merged national interest. The great difference happens to be that these other issues — ruralist grabs for all that may be going in the way of farm subsidies and cheap rural electric power and so on — are not so vital to our continued life as a nation. The ruralists offend where it matters; Megalopolis, in the House, offends where it desperately matters.

This is not, of course, to say that all members from Megalopolis fall into the lowest common denominator of the House. There are currently, for illustration, notable and gallant exceptions to the rule of megalopolitan mediocrity — men like Celler of New York, already mentioned; Lindsay of New York; Frelinghuysen of New Jersey, Reuss of Milwaukee, and a half-dozen others. But it is to say that all schemes for "reforming" Congress through neutralizing its institutional power and simultaneously elevating a so-called "Presidential party" prepared to "work with" the President and based upon urban political power blocs and techniques, would open the gravest risks to the highest interests, as well as the best traditions, of American polity.

These facts of life are constantly accepted within the House itself — and sometimes even by members who academically agree with those who demand basic House reform. They are also invariably accepted, however unwillingly, by wise Presidents, not excluding those whose own short-run partisan designs and programs would theoretically be better served by following the rationale of the innovators.

It is no accident that John F. Kennedy — whose critical mass of popular support came in 1960 from urbanized America — went very slowly, indeed, in associating himself with the extreme demands for House reform arising primarily from urbanized sources. Apart from the circumstance that he himself once served in the House, and so understood the institutional realities there, he had to deal also with the intractable fact that open warfare upon this old Chamber amounts to open warfare upon the whole concept of America as a pluralized society. To break the institution apart, as Franklin D. Roosevelt tried on many occasions to do in hot pursuit of what he earnestly believed to be indispensable legislative actions, would be to flatten that American society beyond its present — and right — degree of homogeneity into something approaching a featureless Peoples Republic. Such a Peoples Republic would not, of course, be "Communist," nor would it be a dictatorship, in the common meaning of that term. It would, however, be a republic in which the political future would belong totally to one of two giant, horizontal, all-national power blocs in which all minority rights, in their old definition, would be not so much denied as simply no longer relevant. To merge the functions and powers of the Presidency with the functions and the then no-longer-existing rights of the House would be to make an outlaw band of the single effectively obstructing force that would thus remain, the United States Senate.

It would be a republic in which great political issues, no matter how complex, no matter how subtle and varicolored, would be settled upon the nakedly simple issue of which of the great contending power blocs could marshal enough people to overrun all other people, without the necessity for civilized compromise or even for political thought, except in its most jejune form. It would be instant government, as in instant coffee.

It will be objected that the purposes of these "reformers" — which, in a word, are a drive for relocating all real Federal power within the Presidency — could not occur without the consent of the people, expressed in their choice of the President. The difficulty with the argument, however, is that it is full of academic logic but lamentably innocent of the higher consideration that free government is essentially illogical.

For it does not follow that a totally free choice of the President by the electorate involves also a totally conscious choice of *legislative* alternatives which may be open in the near or far future. Nor does the notion concern itself with another matter of great pragmatic importance. Suppose the people, in the freest possible choice, elect a certain President and suppose it turns out later that they themselves reckon that they have been wrong in the choice? Is the present possibility of "stalemate" as between Executive and Congress more intolerable than the situation which could occur when, after Congressional reform had struck all real power from the hands of the Capitol, the new repository of all power, the President, was himself found incapable of wise or effective governance?

Reforms fundamentally removing — and not merely altering — Congress' own power of choice (by such devices as making its momentary majority a mere tool in the hands of a President "to whom the people have given their mandate") could do more than temporarily "deadlock" government. They could paralyze government, subject only to the capacity for intervention by the Supreme Court — a body to which the new reformist Majoritarians could hardly rationally turn, since it represents no majority at all and since no one among the citizenry has ever voted upon its membership at all.

All this is instinctively understood by the House. And that is why, granting the occasional instances of excessive dogmatism by committee chairmen, granting the occasional instances of delay and obstructionism, granting the sometimes undue power of the pull of yesterday there, the ultimate strength of the House lies precisely in its hierarchial forms so often criticized. In their details, they are indeed subject to improvement; in their principles they are not wisely subject to abandonment. Nor is the truth of the business a simple option between the views of those who are "liberal" and "forward-looking" and those who are "conservative" and "backward-looking." The truth is not to be found in such puerile concepts.

This is a place of weaknesses as well as of strengths; of delay as well as of decision; of much talk as well as of great actions. But this place — the House of Representatives formed, together with the Senate, into the Congress of the United States — is also something else. It is the people's place; their first and last home in the Federal Republic of the United States of America.

Above all it is a human institution — not a museum; not a monument; not a marble memorial to past grandeurs; but a workshop for the needs of the present and for the necessary plans for the future.

Great men have come and gone here — and some very small men, too — but all have left something which is irreplaceable and timeless. These are the mementos of the long legislative life of this country; the long story of the governance of this country under law.

So this old House is never lifeless, not even when Congress is in recess. Though the shadows of the past fall always over it — where Webster and Lincoln and so many others once walked — the sunshine of the active and urgent here and now is never absent from it, either.

The House is the indispensable link between our public past, our public present and our public future. Humor lives in it. Tragedy lives in it. High endeavor — and sometimes the most earthy of horse trading and logrolling — live in it. For it is a microcosm of the people of the United States themselves — which is what *representative* really means and is — with all their virtues and all their faults; the good, the middling and the bad; the long, the short and the tall.

It is as strong and able as are the people. It is as confused and timid, sometimes, as are the people. It is industrious, and it is tired. It is forward-looking, and it is backward-looking. It is more than the visible symbol of the Union of the States. It *is*, together with the Senate, the Union of the States and, through them, the Union of the People.

INDEX

INDEX

Agriculture Committee, 90
Allen, Leo, 116
Appropriations Committee, 90, 96-97, 120-121
Armed Services Committee, 90, 121-122

Bailey, Cleveland M., 65
Bankhead, William, 97
Banking and Currency Committee, 90
"Board of Education," 45-46
Bolling, Richard, 41-42, 120, 163
Borah, Senator William E., 134
Bradley, Omar, 24-25
Brown, Clarence, 116, 118
Bryce, James, 16-17
Burns, James MacGregor, 155-156

Cannon, Clarence, 121

Cannon, Joseph, 104
Celler, Emanuel, 123-125, 163
Check-and-balance system, 147-148, 151, 152
Civil War. *See* War Between the States
Clay, Henry, 12, 45
Colmer, William, 116, 118, 119
Committee on Committees, 94-95
Committee system, 89-93
Commons, House of. *See* House of Commons
Consensus: method of reaching, 47-153
Curtis, Thomas B., 68

Daily Mirror (London), 154
Dawson, William, 103-104
Debate: in House of Representatives, 25-28
Delaney, James J., 119

Democratic Party, 4, 9-10, 60-61, 69, 73, 94-95, 119

Depression, 47, 59, 131-133, 137

Dirksen, Everett McKinley, 139-140

District of Columbia Committee, 127

Domestic policies: House of Representatives and, 15-16, 39, 43-44, 47, 49

Dulles, John Foster, 66

Education and Labor Committee, 90

Eisenhower, Dwight D., 23-24, 66, 131, 157

Elliott, Carl, 119

Executive Department, 18, 91. *See also* Presidency

Federal system: House of Representatives and, 18-19

Filibuster: Senate and, 108-110, 145

Foreign Affairs Committee, 90-91, 125-127

Foreign policy: House of Representatives and, 47-49, 137-141; Senate and, 39, 44, 47-49, 138, 141

Foreign Relations Committee (Senate), 125

Foster, Augustus, 13-14, 16

Free-Soilers, 9

Frelinghuysen, Peter, Jr., 163

Fulbright, William, 140, 141

Galloway, Dr. George, 13

Garner, John N., 43-44, 45, 83-84, 97, 131

Government Operations Committee, 91

Halleck, Charles, 97, 139-140

Harding, Warren, 134

Hayden, Carl, 121

Hoover, Herbert, 44, 131

House of Commons: House of Representatives and, 16-17, 18-19, 93, 148, 154-155

House of Lords, 12

Hull, Cordell, 36

Hull Reciprocal Tariff, 132

Interior and Insular Affairs Committee, 91

Interstate and Foreign Commerce Committee, 91

Javits, Jacob K., 125

Jefferson, Thomas, 5, 113, 147

Johnson, Andrew, 144

Johnson, Lyndon B., 45, 142-143

Judd, Walter, 64-65, 140

Judiciary Committee, 91-92, 123-124

Kennedy, Edward, 84-85

Kennedy, John F., 36, 49, 68-70, 120, 163

Key districts, 31-34

Kirby, John Henry, 84

Leadership: in House of Representatives, 30-31, 35-37, 39-42, 97-99; in Senate, 34-37
Leadership tables, 11
Lincoln, Abraham, 9-10, 108, 144, 166
Lindsay, John V., 163
Local interests, 54-58, 72
Longworth, Nicholas, 45, 46, 74
Lords, House of. *See* House of Lords

MacArthur, Douglas, 110-111
McCarthy, Joseph, 143-144
McCormack, Edward, 84-85
McCormack, John W., 49, 84-85, 103-104
McElroy, Neil, 65
MacMillan, Harold, 154
McNamara, Robert, 65, 121
Madden, Ray J., 119
Madison, James, 12, 85, 147
Mahon, George, 65-67
Majority party, 11, 18-19
Manchester Guardian, 154
Mansfield, Mike, 141
Marcantonio, Vito, 14-15
Martin, Joseph W., Jr., 80-82, 85
May, Andrew, 98, 99
Members of the House: types of, 5-10, 53-63

Military Affairs Committee, 122
Mills, Wilbur, 36-37, 64
Minority group interests, 161-162, 164
Minority party, 11, 19
Morse, Wayne, 37

National interests, 62-72
Naval Affairs Committee, 122
Nixon, Richard M., 68-69, 70
Norris, George W., 104
Nye, Senator Gerald P., 134

O'Neill, Thomas P., Jr., 120

Paine, Thomas, 13
Parliamentary system: House of Representatives and, 18-19, 153-155
Partisanship, 6, 19-21, 29-30, 77-78, 80, 153-158
Pepper, Claude, 48
Post (Washington), 154
Post Office and Civil Service Committee, 92
Powell, Adam Clayton, 33, 98-99
Presidency: foreign policy and, 138; House of Representatives and, 19-21, 149-150, 152, 155, 156-158, 163; power of, 131-133, 164-165; urban influence and, 4, 159
Prestige: House of Representatives and, 44-45

Public Works Committee, 92

Rankin, John, 14-15
Rayburn, Sam, 23-24, 41-42, 45-47, 49, 60, 74-77, 78, 80-83, 85, 97, 105, 120
Reciprocal Trade Act, 36
Republican Party, 9-10, 60-61, 73, 95-96, 119
Reuss, Henry S., 163
Roosevelt, Eleanor, 84
Roosevelt, Franklin D., 29-30, 47, 59, 60, 61, 74, 75, 84, 131, 132, 134, 155, 163-64
Rules Committee (House), 92, 96-97, 104-120, 144-145, 155
Rules of the House, 12, 41
Rural influence: in House of Representatives, 4-5, 32-34, 113, 159, 162

Sabath, Adolph, 114-117, 118
Science and Astronautics Committee, 92
Senate: debate in, 26, 28; egalitarian attitudes in, 23-24; election of, 31; ex-House members in, 38, 45; filibuster in, 108-110, 145; Foreign Relations Committee of, 125; House of Representatives and, 12-13, 18, 43-49, 72, 133-135, 137, 141, 142-146; leadership in, 34-37, 40, 93; pol-

Senate, cont'd:
icy-making in, 15-16; powers of, 126; prestige of, 43-44; rules of, 35; types of members of, 53-54; urban influence in, 4. See also Foreign policy
Seniority: 22, 31-32, 41, 93, 97-99, 100-104, 143, 155-157
Sisk, B. F., 120
Smith, Howard W., 117, 118, 119
Speaker of the House: power of, 82-85, 95, 97, 104-105; prestige of, 45; mentioned, 11
Standing committees. See Committee system
Statesmanship, 21-22, 108
Stevenson, Adlai E., 103
Structure: of House of Representatives, 32, 89-93
Supreme Court: Congress and, 91, 134-135, 165; seniority and, 99; urban influence in, 4

Taft, Robert A., 48, 116
Taft-Hartley Act, 69
Thomason, R. Ewing, 98, 99
Thornberry, Homer, 119
Times (London), 153
Trimble, James W., 119
Truman, Harry S, 47, 60, 75, 110-111, 114-115, 144, 155

Un-American Activities Committee, 92

Urban influence: in government, 4; in House of Representatives, 4, 9-10, 31-33, 159-163; in Presidency, 4, 159

Veterans Affairs Committee, 92

Vinson, Carl, 121-124

Walsh, Senator Thomas J., 134

War Between the States, 12

Ways and Means Committee, 92, 94-97, 120

Webster, Daniel, 166

Well of the House, 12

Whigs, 9

Wilson, Charles E., 65

Wilson, Woodrow, 74, 106

World War II, 60, 131, 133, 137